Mom Always Said . . .

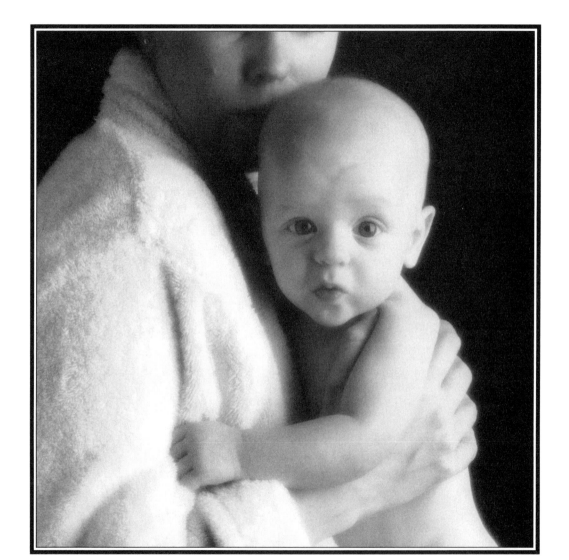

Mom Always Said...

A
COLLECTION
OF
WISDOM, STORIES,
AND SONGS
FOR MOM

EDITED BY CAROL KELLY-GANGI

BARNES
&NOBLE
BOOKS
NEW YORK

Acknowledgments

————— ❊ —————

The editor wishes to thank Rick Campbell, Heather Russell-Revesz, Stuart Miller, and Glorya Hale for their suggestions and expertise.

A special thanks to my family and, as always, to John for all of his love and support.

Dedication

For Mom and John Christopher with love

Table of Contents

PART 2: MOTHER'S HELPER

PART 3: RECIPES FOR MOMS & TOTS

EVERYONE SAYS that nothing changes your life like having a baby. And of course, they're right. There is nothing quite like looking into the face of that little person who you've thought about, waited for, and in many cases longed for, and to think, so this is you. You're finally here and now a new life begins for the both of us. You made me a mother, from the minute I held you in my arms.

Although I'm only 16 months into the mom business, I feel fully entrenched into the club. Our first night home from the hospital found my husband and I huddled over our copy of *What to Expect in the First Year* at 3 a.m. trying to diagnose the little gurgles and yelps erupting out of the cradle. We were happy to discover that our baby was simply doing what newborns do. It's a swift initiation into the world of sleepless nights, diapers, and feedings. But along with the practical side of caring for the new addition to the family, is the wonder and miracle of it all. The bond between mother and child is at once intense, immediate, and all encompassing.

Mom Always Said . . . is for mothers and about mothers. It is part literary reader, part handbook, and part scrapbook. You can refer to it for literature and personal accounts of motherhood, and then share a fairy tale with your child, jot down a favorite recipe, and inscribe your own memories in pages set aside for that purpose.

Each of the literary selections speaks to some aspect of mothers and motherhood. Some contributors reach back to childhood to recall stories and incidents involving their mothers. In "My Oedipus Complex," Frank O'Connor recounts—often hilariously—how his strong bond with his mother was forever altered by his father's sudden return home from World War I. In "The Bird and the Rose," Mary Mackey writes a confession of sorts to her mother where she reveals how as a child she unwittingly broke—and ingeniously repaired—one of her mother's prized possessions. Frederick Douglass pens a moving account of the hardships that his mother endured to see him after being hired out to a distant plantation and the lifelong impact one such visit made upon him.

Other contributors offer personal accounts from their own experience as mothers. Anna Quindlen weighs in on the value of expert opinion in raising children—and how experience is perhaps the best teacher of all. Whoopi Goldberg describes an episode in the age-old battle between teenage daughters and their mothers. Susan Cheever tells the story of her daughter's favorite stuffed animal, and what it came to symbolize for both of them. And Jane Leavy writes a beautiful narrative about the choice to adopt children.

There are also selections from essays, poems, and letters reflecting on the maternal bond. Washington Irving writes candidly about a mother's unconditional love for her children. George Eliot warmly remembers her mother and the "benediction of her gaze." William Butler Yeats compares a mother's never-ending chores with the carefree days of youth. And Louisa May Alcott and her mother, Abigail, exchange letters that reveal their deep love and admiration for one another.

The second part of the book is the *Mother's Helper* section. So when you're done (or dare I say, interrupted) from reading yourself, you can cuddle up with your child to read a fairy tale, sing a lullaby, or even bake some goodies together. The fairy tales include such classics as "Cinderella," "Jack and the Beanstalk," and "Little Red Riding Hood." And the beloved children's songs include many of the perennial favorites that have been enjoyed by children for generations. Completing the collection is a selection of *Recipes for Moms & Tots*—together with pages for recording your own favorite recipes.

Whether you're a new mother or a mother many times over, it is our hope that *Mom Always Said . . .* will be enjoyed by you and your children—and perhaps reveal a glimpse of the inexpressible love and joy that is motherhood.

—CAROL KELLY-GANGI
Rumson, New Jersey

PART 1:
A Mom Is . . .

The Bird and the Rose

By Mary Mackey

Dear Mother,

I have a confession to make: when I was a little girl, about four or five years old, I would wait quietly at the top of the stairs until I heard you chopping onions, taking pots and pans out of the kitchen cabinet, talking on the phone, or cooing to the baby as you bathed him. Then I would slip off my shoes and creep barefoot into your room, crouch down, and open the bottom drawer of your dresser.

As soon as I managed to edge it open, a peculiar, delightful scent would waft out, and I would close my eyes and take deep breaths. It was your scent: a mix of Chanel No. 5 and face powder and sandalwood, and something else, sweet, elusive and voluptuous like your hair freshly washed or your bedtime kiss.

Plunging my hands into the drawer, I would touch the things you had forbidden me to touch. I would run your silk scarves between my fingers; lightly caress your supple arm-length white kid gloves; open a small black box and draw out a cool strand of baroque pearls so pale that they looked like smoke and breath.

In the darkness of your bedroom, in the bottom drawer of that walnut dresser you had refinished with your own hands, all the colors were muted. The reds of your scarves were rust reds, the blues somber, the yellows dim and slightly fragile. Your stockings, neatly boxed and stacked, were as thin as cobwebs, and when I held them up and made them dance, I could see rainbows in them.

You kept many treasures in that drawer—cameos, jet earrings, a gold watch you told me once belonged to my great-grandmother—but the thing I liked best was an ivory pendant about two inches long and one inch wide, delicately carved and fretted like a net. In the center of the pendant, a bird stood on a branch with its head thrust back, singing happily. Above it, the tree blossomed into a pink rose.

I would take out the pendant and touch it against my cheek to feel its gloss. Sometimes I would even lick the pink rose with the tip of my tongue because it looked like the sugar roses you always put on my birthday cakes. The ivory had no taste, of course, but I imagined that I could feel the bird move uneasily as the great child-giant's lips closed above it. Whenever I touched that pendant or made it swing from its black silk cord, I felt happy and powerful and safe, like a traveler who has gone off to some strange, exotic land only to find that all her friends have come with her.

But then, one day, when I was twirling the pendant back and forth, I heard your step on the stairs, and in my panic to get it back in the box and get the drawer shut before you walked in on me, I knocked the bird and its tree against the leg of the dresser, and to my horror it snapped in half. Jamming the broken bits back into the dark cavity of the drawer, I slammed it shut, and crawled under your bed, and sat there watching your feet as I waited for you to discover my crime.

But you discovered nothing, only went to your top drawer to get something—a hair pin perhaps or a handkerchief. When you left again, clicking out of the room in your high heels, I scrambled back to the dresser to try to repair the damage. Since I was only a child, I did not know that time could not be reversed, so at first I simply sat there, holding both halves of the pendant in place, waiting for them to grow back together.

When that failed to happen, I became desperate. If you found out I had been in your drawer and broken one of your prettiest things, you would be angry with me and think I was a bad girl. You might cry the way you cried when Johnny broke your antique fruit dish, or get angry the way you did when I ate a whole bottle of baby aspirin. You might even love me less, and I could never bear that, never. I wanted you to love me—no, I wanted more than that: I wanted to be like you, just like you, wanted to wear those scarves and that scent, to hang that pendant around my neck, to put on those stockings and pearls, to dress myself in silk dresses the way you did, to set a small hat of pheasant feathers on my head, and put your favorite shade of lipstick on my lips.

You were all beauty to me, Mother. You were everything female, everything woman. I loved you so much that I wanted to grow up to be exactly like you; and the thought that I had done something bad, something secret, something sneaking and clumsy choked me with guilt and grief, because I knew you would have never done such a thing when you were a little girl, and that if you discovered these two bits of ivory, this bird snapped in half, you would know that I was not the daughter you loved, but another, worse daughter for whom there was no hope.

I sat for a long time in that dark bedroom, trying to think of how I could mend that pendant, and finally I saw how it could be done. Walking over to Daddy's desk, I took hold of the old straight-backed chair he always sat in and carried it back to the dresser.

Making sure it was secure, I climbed up on the seat and stood for a moment surveying your cut glass jars, your bottles of perfume, your hairbrush and comb. I saw my own guilty face in the mirror, round and big-eyed, my hair straight as a broom, everything distorted by the antique glass. There, right in front of me as I had hoped, was a bottle of clear nail polish.

I had to open that bottle with my teeth, but when I had it open and I was back down at floor level carefully dabbing the point of the brush along the edges of the break, I was filled with a sense of relief and triumph so great that it was all I could do to keep from slopping still more polish onto the bird and the rose.

The polish formed a small, clear line on either side of the fracture, thin as a bit of fingernail, virtually invisible. I took a deep breath, touched the two pieces together and held them, blowing on them and praying that they would stick. At first they kept falling apart, but gradually I began to understand that I had to hold the entire pendant level in the palm of my hand as I pressed.

The room grew darker and the shadow of your closet door crept across the floor. Before it reached my bare feet, the polish turned to glue, and the bird rejoined the tree, and the rectangular net was rewoven. There was only one problem left: a little bit of excess polish that had oozed up through the ivory. Afraid to touch cloth or paper to it, I licked it off. It was sticky and bitter, but I went on, licking like a cat until there was no trace of the clear polish left.

I felt exalted, redeemed, saved. No one could see that the pendant was broken now, not even you. The crack between the two pieces was smaller than a single hair.

This is my confession. I have never told you this story before, but you still have that pendant, Mother, and if you look at it very closely, you will see the bird and the tree and the rose, and the transparent line that runs between them proving how much I have always loved you.

$\mathcal{C}$HILDREN, look into those eyes, listen to the dear voice, notice the feeling of even a single touch that is bestowed upon you by that gentle hand! Make much of it while yet you have that most precious of all good gifts,—a loving mother. Read the unfathomable love of those eyes; the kind anxiety of that tone and look, however slight your pain. In after life you may have friends, fond, dear friends, but never will you have again the inexpressible love and gentleness lavished upon you, which none but mother bestows.

—THOMAS BABINGTON MACAULAY

Hundreds of stars in the pretty sky;
    Hundreds of shells on the shore together;
Hundreds of birds that go singing by;
    Hundreds of bees in the sunny weather.

Hundreds of dewdrops to greet the dawn;
    Hundreds of lambs in the purple clover;
Hundreds of butterflies on the lawn;
    But only one mother the wide world over.

—GEORGE COOPER

My Oedipus Complex

BY FRANK O'CONNOR

FATHER WAS IN THE ARMY ALL THROUGH THE WAR—the first war, I mean—so, up to the age of five, I never saw much of him, and what I saw did not worry me. Sometimes I woke and there was a big figure in khaki peering down at me in the candlelight. Sometimes in the early morning I heard the slamming of the front door and the clatter of nailed boots down the cobbles of the lane. These were Father's entrances and exits. Like Santa Claus he came and went mysteriously.

In fact, I rather liked his visits, though it was an uncomfortable squeeze between Mother and him when I got into the big bed in the early morning. He smoked, which gave him a pleasant musty smell, and shaved, an operation of astounding interest. Each time he left a trail of souvenirs—model tanks and Gurkha knives with handles made of bullet cases, and German helmets and cap badges and button-sticks, and all sorts of military equipment—carefully stowed away in a long box on top of the wardrobe, in case they ever came in handy. There was a bit of the magpie about Father; he expected everything to come in handy. When his back was turned, Mother let me get a chair and rummage through his treasures. She didn't seem to think so highly of them as he did.

The war was the most peaceful period of my life. The window of my attic faced southeast. My mother had curtained it, but that had small effect. I always woke with the first light and, with all the responsibilities of the previous day melted, feeling myself rather like the sun, ready to illumine and rejoice. Life never seemed so simple and clear and full of possibilities as then. I put my feet out from under the clothes— I called them Mrs. Left and Mrs. Right—and invented dramatic situations for them in which they discussed the problems of the day. At least Mrs. Right did; she was very demonstrative, but I hadn't the same control of Mrs. Left, so she mostly contented herself with nodding agreement.

They discussed what Mother and I should do during the day, what Santa Claus should give a fellow for Christmas, and what steps should be taken to brighten the home. There was that little matter of the baby, for instance. Mother and I could never agree about that. Ours was the only house in the terrace without a new baby, and Mother said we couldn't afford one till Father came back from the war because they cost seventeen and six. That showed how simple she was. The Geneys up the road had a baby, and everyone knew they couldn't afford seventeen and six. It was probably a cheap baby, and Mother wanted something really good, but I felt she was too exclusive. The Geneys' baby would have done us fine.

Having settled my plans for the day, I got up, put a chair under the attic window, and lifted the frame high enough to stick out my head. The window overlooked the front gardens of the terrace behind ours, and beyond these it looked over a deep valley to the tall, red-brick houses terraced up the opposite hillside, which were all still in shadow, while those at our side of the valley were all lit up, though with long strange shadows that made them seem unfamiliar; rigid and painted.

After that I went into Mother's room and climbed into the big bed. She woke and I began to tell her of my schemes. By this time, though I never seem to have noticed it, I was petrified in my nightshirt, and I thawed as I talked until, the last frost melted, I fell asleep beside her and woke again only when I heard her below in the kitchen, making the breakfast.

After breakfast we went into town; heard Mass at St. Augustine's and said a prayer for Father, and did the shopping. If the afternoon was fine we either went for a walk in the country or a visit to Mother's great friend in the convent, Mother St. Dominic. Mother had them all praying for Father, and every night, going to bed, I asked God to send him back safe from the war to us. Little, indeed, did I know what I was praying for!

One morning, I got into the big bed, and there, sure enough, was Father in his usual Santa Claus manner, but later, instead of uniform, he put on his best blue suit, and Mother was as pleased as anything. I saw nothing to be pleased about, because, out of uniform, Father was altogether less interesting, but she only beamed, and explained that our prayers had been answered, and off we went to Mass to thank God for having brought Father safely home.

The irony of it! That very day when he came in to dinner he took off his boots and put on his slippers, donned the dirty old cap he wore about the house to save him from colds, crossed his legs, and began to talk gravely to Mother, who looked anxious. Naturally, I disliked her looking anxious, because it destroyed her good looks, so I interrupted him.

"Just a moment, Larry!" she said gently.

This was only what she said when we had boring visitors, so I attached no importance to it and went on talking.

"Do be quiet, Larry!" she said impatiently. "Don't you hear me talking to Daddy?"

This was the first time I had heard those ominous words, "talking to Daddy," and I couldn't help feeling that if this was how God answered prayers, he couldn't listen to them very attentively.

"Why are you talking to Daddy?" I asked with as great a show of indifference as I could muster.

"Because Daddy and I have business to discuss. Now, don't interrupt again!"

In the afternoon, at Mother's request, Father took me for a walk. This time we went into town instead of out the country, and I thought at first, in my usual optimistic way, that it might be an improvement. It was nothing of the sort. Father and I had quite different notions of a walk in town. He had no proper interest in trams, ships, and horses, and the only thing that seemed to divert him was talking to fellows as old as himself. When I wanted to stop he simply went on, dragging me behind him by the hand; when he wanted to stop I had no alternative but to do the same. I noticed that it seemed to be a sign that he wanted to stop for a long time whenever he leaned against a wall. The second time I saw him do it I got wild. He seemed to be settling himself forever. I pulled him by the coat and trousers, but, unlike Mother who, if you were too persistent, got into a wax and said: "Larry, if you don't behave yourself, I'll give you a good slap," Father had an extraordinary capacity for amiable inattention. I sized him up and wondered would I cry, but he seemed to be too remote to be annoyed even by that. Really, it was like going for a walk with a mountain! He either ignored the wrenching and pummeling entirely, or else glanced down with a grin of amusement from his peak. I had never met anyone so absorbed in himself as he seemed.

At teatime, "talking to Daddy" began again, complicated this time by the fact that he had an evening paper, and every few minutes he put it down and told Mother something new out of it. I felt this was foul play. Man for man, I was prepared to compete with him any time for Mother's attention, but when he had it all made up for him by other people it left me no chance. Several times I tried to change the subject without success.

"You must be quiet when Daddy is reading, Larry," Mother said impatiently.

It was clear that she either genuinely liked talking to Father better than talking to me, or else that he had some terrible hold on her which made her afraid to admit the truth.

"Mummy," I said that night when she was tucking me up, "do you think if I prayed hard God would send Daddy back to the war?"

She seemed to think about that for a moment.

"No, dear," she said with a smile. "I don't think he would."

"Why wouldn't he, Mummy?"

"Because there isn't a war any longer, dear."

"But, Mummy, couldn't God make another war, if He liked?"

"He wouldn't like to, dear. It's not God who makes wars, but bad people."

"Oh!" I said.

I was disappointed about that. I began to think that God wasn't quite what he was cracked up to be.

Next morning I woke at my usual hour, feeling like a bottle of champagne. I put out my feet and invented a long conversation in which Mrs. Right talked of the trouble she had with her own father till she put him in the Home. I didn't quite know what the Home was but it sounded the right place for Father. Then I got my chair and stuck my head out of the attic window. Dawn was just breaking, with a guilty air that made me feel I had caught it in the act. My head bursting with stories and schemes, I stumbled in next door, and in the half-darkness scrambled into the big bed. There was no room at Mother's side so I had to get between her and Father. For the time being I had forgotten about him, and for several minutes I sat bolt upright, racking my brains to know what I could do with him. He was taking up more than his fair share of the bed, and I couldn't get comfortable, so I gave him several kicks that made him grunt and stretch. He made room all right, though. Mother waked and felt for me. I settled back comfortably in the warmth of the bed with my thumb in my mouth.

"Mummy!" I hummed, loudly and contentedly.

"Sssh! dear," she whispered. "Don't wake Daddy!"

This was a new development, which threatened to be even more serious than "talking to Daddy." Life without my early-morning conferences was unthinkable.

"Why?" I asked severely.

"Because poor Daddy is tired."

This seemed to me a quite inadequate reason, and I was sickened by the sentimentality of her "poor Daddy." I never liked that sort of gush; it always struck me as insincere.

"Oh!" I said lightly. Then in my most winning tone: "Do you know where I want to go with you today, Mummy?"

"No, dear," she sighed.

"I want to go down the Glen and fish for thornybacks with my new net, and then I went to go out to the Fox and Hounds, and—"

"Don't-wake-Daddy!" she hissed angrily, clapping her hand across my mouth.

But it was too late. He was awake, or nearly so. He grunted and reached for the matches. Then he stared incredulously at his watch.

"Like a cup of tea, dear?" asked Mother in a meek, hushed voice I had never heard her use before. It sounded almost as though she were afraid.

"Tea?" he exclaimed indignantly. "Do you know what the time is?"

"And after that I want to go up the Rathcooney Road," I said loudly, afraid I'd forget something in all those interruptions.

"Go to sleep at once, Larry!" she said sharply.

I began to snivel. I couldn't concentrate, the way that pair went on, and smothering my early-morning schemes was like burying a family from the cradle.

Father said nothing, but lit his pipe and sucked it, looking out into the shadows without minding Mother or me. I knew he was mad. Every time I made a remark Mother hushed me irritably. I was mortified. I felt it wasn't fair; there was even something sinister in it. Every time I had pointed out to her the waste of making two beds when we could both sleep in one, she had told me it was healthier like that, and now here was this man, this stranger, sleeping with her without the least regard for her health!

He got up early and made tea, but though he brought Mother a cup he brought none for me.

"Mummy," I shouted, "I want a cup of tea, too."

"Yes, dear," she said patiently. "You can drink from Mummy's saucer."

That settled it. Either Father or I would have to leave the house. I didn't want to drink from Mother's saucer; I wanted to be treated as an equal in my own home, so, just to spite her, I drank it all and left none for her. She took that quietly, too.

But that night when she was putting me to bed she said gently:

"Larry, I want you to promise me something."

"What is it?" I asked.

"Not to come in and disturb poor Daddy in the morning. Promise?"

"Poor Daddy" again! I was becoming suspicious of everything involving that quite impossible man.

"Why?" I asked.

"Because poor Daddy is worried and tired and he doesn't sleep well."

"Why doesn't he, Mummy?"

"Well, you know, don't you, that while he was at the war Mummy got the pennies from the Post Office?"

"From Miss MacCarthy?"

"That's right. But now, you see, Miss MacCarthy hasn't any more pennies, so Daddy must go out and find us some. You know what would happen if he couldn't?"

"No," I said, "tell us."

"Well, I think we might have to go out and beg for them like the poor old woman on Fridays. We wouldn't like that, would we?"

"No," I agreed. "We wouldn't."

"So you'll promise not to come in and wake him?"

"Promise."

Mind you, I meant that. I knew pennies were a serious matter, and I was all against having to go out and beg like the old woman on Fridays. Mother laid out all my toys in a complete ring round the bed so that, whatever way I got out, I was bound to fall over one of them.

When I woke I remembered my promise all right. I got up and sat on the floor and played—for hours, it seemed to me. Then I got my chair and looked out the attic window for more hours. I wished it was time for Father to wake; I wished someone would make me a cup of tea. I didn't feel in the least like the sun; instead, I was bored and so

very, very cold! I simply longed for the warmth and depth of the big featherbed.

At last I could stand it no longer. I went into the next room. As there was still no room at Mother's side I climbed over her and she woke with a start.

"Larry," she whispered, gripping my arm very tightly, "what did you promise?"

"But I did, Mummy," I wailed, caught in the very act. "I was quiet for ever so long."

"Oh, dear, and you're perished!" she said sadly, feeling me all over. "Now, if I let you stay will you promise not to talk?"

"But I want to talk, Mummy," I wailed.

"That has nothing to do with it," she said with a firmness that was new to me. "Daddy wants to sleep. Now, do you understand that?"

I understood it only too well. I wanted to talk, he wanted to sleep—whose house was it, anyway?

"Mummy," I said with equal firmness, "I think it would be healthier for Daddy to sleep in his own bed."

That seemed to stagger her, because she said nothing for a while.

"Now, once for all," she went on, "you're to be perfectly quiet or go back to your own bed. Which is it to be?"

The injustice of it got me down. I had convicted her out of her own mouth of inconsistency and unreasonableness, and she hadn't even attempted to reply. Full of spite, I gave Father a kick, which she didn't notice but which made him grunt and open his eyes in alarm.

"What time is it?" he asked in a panic-stricken voice, not looking at Mother but at the door, as if he saw someone there.

"It's early yet," she replied soothingly. "It's only the child. Go to sleep again . . . Now, Larry," she added, getting out of bed, "you've wakened Daddy and you must go back."

This time, for all her quiet air, I knew she meant it, and knew that my principal rights and privileges were as good as lost unless I asserted them at once. As she lifted me, I gave a screech, enough to wake the dead, not to mind Father. He groaned.

"That damn child! Doesn't he ever sleep?"

"It's only a habit, dear," she said quietly, though I could see she was vexed.

"Well, it's time he got out of it," shouted Father, beginning to heave in the bed. He suddenly gathered all the bedclothes about him, turned to the wall, and then looked back over his shoulder with nothing showing only two small, spiteful, dark eyes. The man looked very wicked.

To open the bedroom door, Mother had to let me down, and I broke free and dashed for the farthest corner, screeching. Father sat bolt upright in bed.

"Shut up, you little puppy!" he said in a choking voice.

I was so astonished that I stopped screeching. Never, never had anyone spoken to me in that tone before. I looked at him incredulously and saw his face convulsed with rage. It was only then that I fully realized how God had codded me, listening to my prayers for the safe return of this monster.

"Shut up, you!" I bawled, beside myself.

"What's that you said?" shouted Father, making a wild leap out of the bed.

"Mick, Mick!" cried Mother. "Don't you see the child isn't used to you?"

"I see he's better fed than taught," snarled Father, waving his arms wildly. "He wants his bottom smacked."

All his previous shouting was as nothing to these obscene words referring to my person. They really made my blood boil.

"Smack your own!" I screamed hysterically. "Smack your own! Shut up! Shut up!"

At this he lost his patience and let fly at me. He did it with the lack of conviction you'd expect of a man under Mother's horrified eyes, and it ended up as a mere tap, but the sheer indignity of being struck at all by a stranger, a total stranger who had cajoled his way back from the war into our big bed as a result of my innocent intercession, made me completely dotty. I shrieked and shrieked, and danced in my bare feet, and Father, looking awkward and hairy in nothing but a short gray army shirt, glared down at me like a mountain out for murder. I think it must have been then that I realized he was jealous too. And there stood Mother in her nightdress, looking as if her heart was broken between us. I hoped she felt as she looked. It seemed to me that she deserved it all.

From that morning out my life was a hell. Father and I were enemies, open and avowed. We conducted a series of skirmishes against one another, he trying to steal my time with Mother and I his. When she was sitting on my bed, telling me a story, he took to looking for some pair of old boots which he alleged he had left behind him at the beginning of the war. While he talked to Mother I played loudly with my toys to show my total lack of concern. He created a terrible scene one evening when he came in from work and found me at his box, playing with his regimental badges, Gurkha knives and buttonsticks. Mother got up and took the box from me.

"You mustn't play with Daddy's toys unless he lets you, Larry," she said severely. "Daddy doesn't play with yours."

For some reason Father looked at her as if she had struck him and then turned away with a scowl.

"Those are not toys," he growled, taking down the box again to see had I lifted anything. "Some of those curios are very rare and valuable."

But as time went on I saw more and more how he managed to alienate Mother and me. What made it worse was that I couldn't grasp his method or see what attraction he had for Mother. In every possible way he was less winning than I. He had a common accent and made noises at his tea. I thought for a while that it might be the newspapers she was interested in, so I made up bits of news of my own to read to her. Then I thought it might be the smoking, which I personally thought attractive, and took his pipes and went round the house dribbling into them till he caught me. I even made noises at my tea, but Mother only told me I was disgusting. It all seemed to hinge round that unhealthy habit of sleeping together, so I made a point of dropping into their bedroom and nosing round, talking to myself, so that they wouldn't know I was watching them, but they were never up to anything that I could see. In the end it beat me. It seemed to depend on being grown-up and giving people rings, and I realized I'd have to wait.

But at the same time I wanted him to see that I was only waiting, not giving up the fight. One evening when he was being particularly obnoxious, chattering away well above my head, I let him have it.

"Mummy," I said, "do you know what I'm going to do when I grow up?"

"No, dear," she replied. "What?"

"I'm going to marry you," I said quietly.

Father gave a great guffaw out of him, but he didn't take me in. I knew it must only be pretense. And Mother, in spite of everything, was pleased. I felt she was probably relieved to know that one day Father's hold on her would be broken.

"Won't that be nice?" she said with a smile.

"It'll be very nice," I said confidently. "Because we're going to have lots and lots of babies."

"That's right, dear," she said placidly. "I think we'll have one soon, and then you'll have plenty of company."

I was no end pleased about that because it showed that in spite of the way she gave in to Father she still considered my wishes. Besides, it would put the Geneys in their place.

It didn't turn out like that, though. To begin with, she was very preoccupied—I supposed about where she would get the seventeen and six—and though Father took to staying out late in the evenings it did me no particular good. She stopped taking me for walks, became as touchy as blazes, and smacked me for nothing at all. Sometimes I wished I'd never mentioned the confounded baby—I seemed to have a genius for bringing calamity on myself.

And calamity it was! Sonny arrived in the most appalling hullabaloo—even that much he couldn't do without a fuss—and from the first moment I disliked him. He was a difficult child—so far as I was concerned he was always difficult—and demanded far too much attention. Mother was simply silly about him, and couldn't see when he was only showing off. As company he was worse than useless. He slept all day, and I had to go round the house on tiptoe to avoid waking him. It wasn't any longer a question of not waking Father. The slogan now was "Don't-wake-Sonny!" I couldn't understand why the child wouldn't sleep at the proper time, so whenever Mother's back was turned I woke him. Sometimes to keep him awake I pinched him as well. Mother caught me at it one day and gave me a most unmerciful flaking.

One evening when Father was coming in from work, I was playing trains in the front garden. I let on not to notice him; instead, I pretended to be talking to myself, and said in a loud voice: "If any other bloody baby comes into this house, I'm going out."

Father stopped dead and looked at me over his shoulder.

"What's that you said?" he asked sternly.

"I was only talking to myself," I replied, trying to conceal my panic. "It's private."

He turned and went in without a word. Mind you, I intended it as a solemn warning, but its effect was quite different. Father started being quite nice to me. I could understand that, of course. Mother was quite sickening about Sonny. Even at mealtimes she'd get up and gawk at him in the cradle with an idiotic smile, and tell Father to do the same. He was always polite about it, but he looked so puzzled you could see he didn't know what she was talking about. He complained of the way Sonny cried at night, but she only got cross and said that Sonny never cried except when there was something up with him—which was a flaming lie, because Sonny never had anything up with him, and only cried for attention. It was really painful to see how simple-minded she was. Father wasn't attractive, but he had a fine intelligence. He saw through Sonny, and now he knew that I saw through him as well.

One night I woke with a start. There was someone beside me in the bed. For one wild moment I felt sure it must be Mother, having come to her senses and left Father for good, but then I heard Sonny in convulsions in the next room, and Mother saying: "There! There! There!" and I knew it wasn't she. It was Father. He was lying beside me, wide awake, breathing hard and apparently as mad as hell.

After a while it came to me what he was mad about. It was his turn now. After turning me out of the big bed, he had been turned out himself. Mother had no consideration now for anyone but that poisonous pup, Sonny. I couldn't help feeling sorry for Father. I had been through it all myself, and even at that age I was magnanimous. I began to stroke him down and say: "There! There!" he wasn't exactly responsive.

"Aren't you asleep either?" he snarled.

"Ah, come on and put your arm around us, can't you?" I said, and he did, in a sort of way. Gingerly, I suppose, is how you'd describe it. He was very bony but better than nothing.

At Christmas he went out of his way to buy me a really nice model railway.

A Mother's love is the golden link

Binding youth to age;

And he is still but a child,

However time may have furrowed his cheek,

Who cannot happily recall, with a softened heart,

The fond devotion and gentle chidings

Of the best friend God ever gave.

—CHRISTIAN BOVÉE

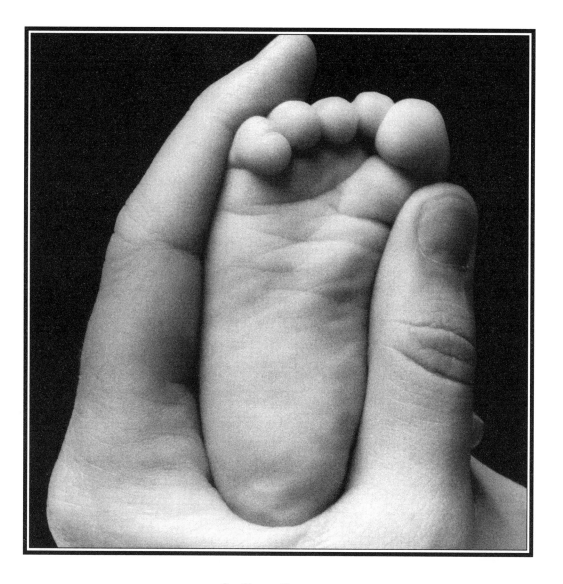

The American Woman as a Mother

BY THEODORE ROOSEVELT

NO ORDINARY WORK DONE by a man is either as hard or as responsible as the work of a woman who is bringing up a family of small children; for upon her time and strength demands are made not only every hour of the day but often every hour of the night. She may have to get up night after night to take care of a sick child, and yet must by day continue to do all her household duties as well; and if the family means are scant she must usually enjoy even her rare holidays taking her whole brood of children with her. The birth pangs make all men the debtors of all women. Above all, our sympathy and regard are due to the struggling wives among

those whom Abraham Lincoln called the plain people, and whom he so loved and trusted; for the lives of these women are often led on the lonely heights of quiet, self-sacrificing heroism. . . . The woman's task is not easy—no task worth doing is easy—but in doing it, and when she has done it, there shall come to her the highest and holiest joy known to mankind; and having done it, she shall have the reward prophesied in Scripture: for her husband and her children, yes, and all people who realize that her work lies at the foundation of all national happiness and greatness, shall rise up and call her blessed.

Real Me

BY SUSAN CHEEVER

WHEN MY DAUGHTER WAS BORN EIGHTEEN YEARS AGO, my brother Fred and his wife sent her a stuffed brown bear with a white nose and tummy and a manufacturer's name tag which told us its name was "Snuffles." Snuffles joined the piles of plush bears, dogs, cats, frogs, and clowns in her room; she was my first child and my parents' first granddaughter, two facts which seemed to provoke stuffed animal buying orgies on the part of otherwise sensible people. But slowly, as she grew and learned to grab, cuddle, and express preferences, she gravitated toward Snuffles. As soon as she could gesture, she let us know that Snuffles needed to be in her crib at night. She began regularly falling asleep with her tiny hands nestling in the bear's soft fur. Like all first-time mothers, I had read every baby book from Dr. Spock and Penelope Leach to Margaret Mahler, and I knew that the bear was my daughter's transitional object. I was proud of everything she did, and settling on such an appealing transitional object seemed further evidence of her exceptional intelligence.

Of course she didn't call the bear Snuffles. She was ten months old and innocent of the silly names provided by manufacturers for their products. She didn't even realize it was a bear. She thought it was a male cat and she called it Meow, which she shorted to Me. Me the bear became her most beloved thing, the center of her secure world. "Where's my Me?" she would ask, in her sweet little voice. "Where's Me?"

What the baby books forgot to mention was the devastating effect of too much love. By the time my daughter was two years old, Me was worn and tattered from being caressed, his once gleaming fur had been fondled to a dull, tufted fabric, his button eyes were missing, and his smile kissed away. After a citywide hunt, I located another Me—a new Snuffles—and brought him home triumphantly. My daughter was less than pleased. She added the new bear to her menagerie and continued to sleep with the worn-out old one, amending his name to "Real Me" to distinguish him from the imposter.

By the time my daughter turned three, Real Me was a sorry sight. As he became more tattered, he seemed to become more necessary—especially after my daughter gave up the bottle which had lulled her to sleep. She couldn't even think about bedtime until Real Me was ensconced on her pillow. When we traveled, Real Me was the first thing I packed. As he crumbled, my anxieties soared. What if he was lost? What if he just came apart at the seams one day after a particularly energetic hug? I was convinced that if that happened my daughter would never sleep again. When I slept, I sometimes had nightmares about Real Me. In my dreams he disappeared or disintegrated as I watched helplessly. My psychiatrist asked if I thought my marriage was disintegrating.

One day, shopping in a downtown department store, the escalator took me past the toy department. There, displayed as if he was meant for me to see, was another new Snuffles. This time, I had him wrapped in plain brown paper. That night while my little girl slept, I massacred this new Snuffles with a pair of scissors, reducing him to parts-—yes, nose, ears, and swatches of fur. I crept into her bedroom and stealthily took Real Me from her pillow. With an ear cocked toward the room where she innocently dreamed, I hastily sewed on one new plush leg.

I had a restless night. Had I tampered with the thing my daughter cared about the most, and ruined it forever? Had I failed to respect her feelings for the one object in the household which belonged to her and her alone? Would she notice and be horrified? The next morning I held my breath. She didn't comment. That night at bedtime, I watched terrified as she stroked the new leg in her sleepy ritual. "Mmmm, soft," she said. After that, every few weeks, I replaced a tiny part of Real Me with a part from the new Snuffles. I have continued to replace parts of Real Me with dozens of parts from new Snuffleses I have bought over the years. After a few years, my daughter realized what was happening, but by then my replacement rituals had become as much a part of Real Me as the bear himself, and she accepted the fact that he was a patchwork of old and new.

Real Me sits on my computer as I write this, one-eyed and tattered, his tail all but worn off. It's been a few years since I have replaced a part. As he is fondled less, he wears better. My daughter is with her father this weekend (our marriage was disintegrating). These days Real Me sleeps at the end of her bed in a pile of quilts. She doesn't notice him much, and when she leaves she doesn't take him with her. Her security comes from other things now. I still keep him though: he's a memento of that time long ago when my teenager was a baby, and a proof that although too much love can destroy, it can also repair and mend.

Describe a favorite stuffed animal or cherished toy from your childhood. Who gave it to you? What ever happened to it?

_____

_____

_____

_____

_____

_____

_____

_____

_____

_____

_____

_____

_____

_____

_____

_____

Women know

The way to rear up children (to be just)

They have a merry, simple, tender knack

Of trying sashes, fitting babies' shoes,

And stringing pretty words that make no sense,

And kissing full sense into empty words;

Which things are corals to cut life upon

Although such trifles.

—ELIZABETH BARRETT BROWNING

Goodbye, Dr. Spock

BY ANNA QUINDLEN

I F NOT FOR THE PHOTOGRAPHS I might have a hard time believing they ever existed. The pensive infant with the swipe of dark bangs and the black button eyes of a Raggedy Andy doll. The placid baby with the yellow ringlets and the high piping voice. The sturdy toddler with the lower lip that curled into an apostrophe above her chin.

All my babies are gone now. I say this not in sorrow but in disbelief. I take great satisfaction in what I have today: three almost-adults, two taller than I am, one closing in fast. Three people who read the same books I do and have learned not to be afraid of disagreeing with me in their opinion of them, who sometimes tell vulgar jokes that make me laugh until I choke up and cry, who need razor blades and shower gel and privacy, who want to keep their doors closed more than I like. Who, miraculously, go to the bathroom, zip up their jackets and move food from plate to mouth all by themselves. Like the trick soap I bought for the bathroom with a rubber duckie at its center, the baby is buried deep within each, barely discernible except through the unreliable haze of the past.

Everything in all the books I once pored over is finished for me now. Penelope Leach. T. Berry Brazelton. Dr. Spock. The ones on sibling rivalry and sleeping through the night and early-childhood education, all grown obsolete. Along with "Goodnight Moon" and "Where the Wild Things Are," they are battered, spotted, well used. But I suspect that if you flipped the pages dust would rise like memories.

What those books taught me, finally, and what the women on the playground taught me, and the well-meaning relations—what they taught me was that they couldn't really teach me very much at all. Raising children is presented at first as a true-false test, then becomes multiple choice, until finally, far along, you realize that it is an endless essay. No one knows anything. One child responds well to positive reinforcement, another can be managed only with a stern voice and a timeout. One boy is toilet trained at 3, his brother at 2. When my first child was born, parents were told to put Baby to bed on his belly so that he would not choke on his own spit-up. By the time my last arrived, babies were put down on their backs because of research on sudden infant death syndrome.

To a new parent this ever-shifting certainty is terrifying, and then soothing. Eventually you must learn to trust yourself. Eventually the research will follow. First science told us they were insensate blobs. But we thought they were looking, and

watching, and learning, even when they spent so much time hitting themselves in the face. And eventually science said that we were right, that important cognitive function began in early babyhood. First science said environment was the great shaper of human nature. But it certainly seemed as though those babies had distinct personalities, some contemplative, some gregarious, some crabby. And eventually science said that was right, too, and that they were hard-wired exactly as we had suspected.

Still, the temptation to defer to the experts was huge. The literate parent, who approaches everything—cooking, decorating, life—as though there were a paper due or an exam scheduled, is in particular peril when the kids arrive. How silly it all seems now, the obsessing about language acquisition and physical milestones, the riding the waves of normal, gifted, hyperactive, all those labels that reduced individuality to a series of cubbyholes. But I could not help myself. I had watched my mother casually raise five children born over 10 years, but by watching her I intuitively knew that I was engaged in the greatest—and potentially most catastrophic—task of my life. I knew that there were mothers who had worried with good reason, that there were children who would have great challenges to meet. We were lucky; ours were not among them. Nothing horrible or astonishing happened: there was hernia surgery, some stitches, a broken arm and a fuchsia cast to go with it.

Mostly ours were the ordinary everyday terrors and miracles of raising a child, and our children's challenges the old familiar ones of learning to live as themselves in the world. The trick was to get past my fears, my ego and my inadequacies to help them do that. During my first pregnancy I picked up a set of old clothbound books at a flea market. Published in 1933, they were called "Mother's Encyclopedia," and one volume described what a mother needs to be: "psychologically good: sound, wholesome, healthy, unafraid, able to deal with the world and to live in this particular age, an integrated personality, an adjusted person." In a word, yow.

It is good that we know so much more now, know that mothers need not be perfect to be successful. But some of what we learn is as pernicious as that daunting description, calculated to make us feel like failures every single day. I remember 15 years ago poring over one of Dr. Brazelton's wonderful books on child development, in which he describes three different sorts of infants: average, quiet and active. I was looking for a subquiet codicil (see: slug) for an 18-month-old who did not walk. Was there something wrong with his fat little legs? Was there something wrong with his tiny little mind? Was he developmentally delayed, physically challenged? Was I insane? Last year he went to China. Next year he goes to college. He can walk just fine. He can walk too well. Every part of raising children at some point comes down to this: be careful what you wish for.

Every part of raising children is humbling, too. Believe me, mistakes were made. They have all been enshrined in the "Remember When Mom Did" Hall of Fame. The outbursts, the temper tantrums, the bad language—mine, not theirs. The times the baby fell off the bed. The times I arrived late for preschool pickup. The nightmare sleepover. The horrible summer camp. The day when the youngest came barreling out of the classroom with a 98 on her geography test, and I responded, "What did you get wrong?" (She insisted I include that.) The time I ordered food at the McDonald's drive-through speaker and then drove away without picking it up from the window. (They all insisted I include that.) I did not allow them to watch "The Simpsons" for the first two seasons. What was I thinking?

But the biggest mistake I made is the one that most of us make while doing this. I did not live in the moment enough. This is particularly clear now that the moment is gone, captured only in photographs. There is one picture of the three of them sitting in the grass on a quilt in the shadow of the swing set on a summer day, ages 6, 4 and 1. And I wish I could remember what we ate, and what we talked about, and how they sounded, and how they looked when they slept that night. I wish I had not been in such a hurry to get on to the next thing: dinner, bath, book, bed. I wish I had treasured the doing a little more and the getting it done a little less.

Even today I'm not sure what worked and what didn't, what was me and what was simply life. How much influence did I really have over the personality of the former baby who cried only when we gave parties and who today, as a teenager, still dislikes socializing and crowds? When they were very small, I suppose I thought someday they would become who they were because of what I'd done. Now I suspect they simply grew into their true selves because they demanded in a thousand ways that I back off and let them be.

There was babbling I forgot to do, stimulation they never got, foods I meant to introduce and never got around to introducing. If a black-and-white mobile really increases depth perception and early exposure to classical music increases the likelihood of perfect pitch, I blew it. The books said to be relaxed and I was often tense, matter-of-fact and I was sometimes over the top. And look how it all turned out. I wound up with the three people I like best in the world, who have done more than anyone to excavate my essential humanity. That's what the books never told me. I was bound and determined to learn from the experts. It just took me a while to figure out who the experts were.

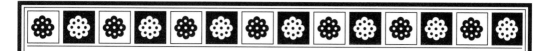

Our mother bade us keep the trodden ways,
Stroked down my tippet, set my brother's frill,
Then with the benediction of her gaze,
Clung to us lessening and pursued us still
Across the homestead to the rookery elms
Whose tall old trunks had each a grassy mound,
So rich for us, we counted them as realms
With varied products; here were earth nuts found
And here the Lady-fingers, in deep shade,
Here sloping toward the moat the rushes grew,
The large to split for pith, the small to braid
While over all the dark rooks cawing flew
And made a happy strange solemnity
A deep-toned chant from life unknown to me.

—GEORGE ELIOT

PHOTO MEMORIES

Take out a favorite photograph of you and your children when they were young. Paste it here and write down everything you can think of about that time with them.

Dear Daughter,

Your tenth birthday has arrived. May it be a happy one, and on each returning birthday may you feel new strength and resolution to be gentle with sisters, obedient to parents, loving to everyone, and happy in yourself.

I give you the pencil-case I promised, for I have observed that you are fond of writing, and wish to encourage the habit.

Go on trying, dear, and each day it will be easier to be and do good. You must help yourself, for the cause of your little troubles is in yourself; and patience and courage only will make you what Mother prays to see you—her good and happy girl.

—ABIGAIL ALCOTT
in a letter to her daughter Louisa, 1839

Dear Mother,

Into your Christmas stocking I have put my "first-born," knowing that you will accept it with all its faults (for grandmothers are always kind), and look upon it merely as an earnest of what I may yet do; for, with so much to cheer me on, I hope to pass in time from fairies and fables to men and realities.

Whatever beauty or poetry is to be found in my little book is owing to your interest in and encouragement of all my efforts from the first to the last; and if ever I do anything to be proud of, my greatest happiness will be that I can thank you for that, as I may do for all the good there is in me; and I shall be content to write if it gives you pleasure. . . .

I am ever your loving daughter,

Louy

—**Louisa May Alcott,**
in a letter to her mother, Christmas, 1854

$\mathcal{A}$ MOTHER is the truest friend we have, when trials, heavy and sudden, fall upon us; when adversity takes the place of prosperity; when friends who rejoice with us in our sunshine, desert us when troubles thicken around us, still will she cling to us, and endeavor by her kind precepts and counsels to dissipate the clouds of darkness, and cause peace to return to our hearts. . . . But a mother's love endures through all; in good repute, in bad repute, in the face of the world's condemnation, a mother still loves on, and still hopes that her child may turn from his evil ways, and repent; still she remembers the infant smiles that once filled her bosom with rapture, the merry laugh, the joyful shout of his childhood, the opening promise of his youth; and she can never be brought to think him all unworthy.

—WASHINGTON IRVING

BY WHOOPI GOLDBERG

ONE NIGHT when my kid was maybe thirteen or fourteen, she came downstairs wearing three pieces of cloth. She said she was going out, and it was none of my business where. I looked this child over, this little version of me. The cloth itself was all shiny and nice and fine, but it wasn't covering enough to suit a mother. It wasn't even close. It was probably against the law, in some states, to go out looking like she wanted to go out looking. Okay, in my time I wore a mini so small that all I needed to do was sneeze and you would have known exactly what color my panties were, but here was my barely teenage daughter, looking like a grown woman, dressed like Madonna used to dress. I completely flipped.

Before my mother could come out of my mouth, she was in my ear. I heard her chuckling in the corner, laughing at me over the way our situation had turned. This was parental justice. Her laugh took me back, and pissed me off. "Why are you laughing?" I shot back.

"Because it's funny," she said. "Because it's funny to see you like this now."

Funny? I'm trying to explain to this child that she can't go out looking like this. She can't go out looking like this because you don't know what invitation someone is going to pick up from this.

That line—you don't know what invitation someone is going to pick up from this—was one of my mother's, and I wanted to suck it right back into my face as soon as I'd said it. My mother looked over at me and smiled, and at first I tried not to smile back, but it was too late. I had to smile too. It wasn't one of those let-me-laugh-along-with-you kinda smiles, or one of those gee-ain't-we-funny kinda smiles, but the kind of smile that comes from knowing. I got it.

Finally. I understood. It was a smile of recognition, and maybe a little surrender. I reconnected to everything that had passed between us, and I could see what was coming. I wanted to tell my mother how sorry I was for putting her through all those motions, for not recognizing that she had something to offer beyond what I could see. But she knew. She smiled back and she knew.

I turned to my kid and said, "You know what? Go out. Just go." And she did. She looked at me kinda funny, and suspicious, but she went out like she'd planned. And then she came back, about twenty minutes later. "You know what?" she said. "It's cold out there. I think I'm gonna change, put a little more on."

It happens, but it takes time. I watch now as my daughter goes through it for herself, with her own kids, and I try not to chuckle. She'll hear me coming out of her mouth and she'll look over with one of those knowing smiles and start to laugh, because we all get it, eventually.

When I was young, my mother and I . . .

_____

_____

_____

_____

_____

_____

_____

_____

_____

_____

_____

_____

_____

_____

_____

My Choice

BY JANE LEAVY

ONE DAY WHEN MY DAUGHTER WAS A TULIP, the name given to the oldest children in her florally-arranged preschool, she came home with exciting news.

"This is Being Born Week! Three pregnant moms will be visiting our class to talk about becoming a mother! Please bring in Your Coming Home Story and a picture of yourself as a newborn!"

As the mother of two adopted children, Emma and her older brother, Nick, I was touched by the teacher's upbeat inclusiveness, her perky sensitivity to what are sometimes called "options in family building." After all, coming home is something we all do, no matter who's responsible for the legwork of labor and delivery.

Infused with goodwill, I picked up the phone and called the teacher. "I'm sure you have an adoptive parent to talk to the kids," I said, knowing that one fifth of the children in her class were adopted, including those of the director and assistant director of the school. "But if not, I'm available."

The teacher replied that I was neither welcome nor needed in the Tulip Room. "This is not family week," she said, firmly. "This is about biology."

It occurred to me, but only later, the way things do, to question why she was teaching four-year-olds about reproduction. My immediate reaction was stunned disbelief: I'd been banished from the Tulip Room. And in banishing me, the teacher had ensured that my daughter would be an exile among Tulips.

I appeared to the assistant director for help. She demurred, saying she could not intervene without undermining pedagogical autonomy. I demurred, saying no one in a position of authority was going to teach my children that motherhood is defined solely by biology.

I was surprised by my ferocity, as was she. Clearly something fundamental had been mobilized inside. Something I'd been avoiding since the day our first child came home to us: the whole raw complex of nerve endings associated with the word *motherhood*.

The inability to reproduce is a monthly kind of death. Each new moon brings hope, then despair. Oddly, it isn't hope that makes you keep trying, but the opposite. The more you invest in the effort to procreate, the more essential it becomes. Each time my body said no, my heart said, *I can't be going through all this for nothing*. But you can, and we did. Month after month, grief compounded like interest. The embryonic need to reproduce grew—it was the only thing that grew—until it got so big we forgot this wasn't about our gene pool but about becoming parents.

If you're lucky, and I was, a friend will point this out to you. If you're unlucky, she may be pregnant at the time. I hated Diana for having a baby. I hated her more for telling me I should adopt one. And I hated hearing it from her as much as I admire her now for saying it.

The day after our last failed in vitro fertilization cycle, we filled out an application to adopt.

Choice is a loaded word in the modern lexicon of motherhood. But it has a special meaning for me. Accidents don't happen in adoption—it is a concerted decision. And, like most other life choices, it carries special responsibilities and complications, among them the privilege of choosing the gender of your child.

I never doubted I could raise a boy. I liked the idea of being a feminist mom to a macho son. After all, I grew up perfecting Mickey Mantle's swing. Red Barber's muffled voice coming to me through a pillow was my idea of a lullaby. Other girls wore party shoes on the first day of school. I saved my Mary Janes for the first day of the baseball season.

We asked for a boy. A month and a half after filling out the papers, we had a son, a gestation period of exactly six weeks.

The call came late on a Friday afternoon, the last day of a Cape Cod vacation. We were packing up, happily finishing off what was left of the summer rum. A female voice on the other end of the phone said, "There's a little boy waiting for you in Phoenix."

Being a reporter, I took notes on the conversation. I knew I'd never remember anything else she said. After we hung up, we went into town to buy a book, *Name Your Baby*. We chose our son's name by the lake shore: Nicholas *Ariel*, which he hates and I love. His is our airy sprite.

The drive home was a blur; 100 mph all the way down the New Jersey Turnpike. After four years of humiliating fertility treatments, some no more scientific than animal husbandry, we were ready to be parents—which is a whole different thing from being prepared.

On Monday morning, Federal Express delivered a set of baby pictures to my office. I showed them around like any other proud new parent. I just happened to be one who hadn't seen her child. I don't remember thinking that was strange. I remember thinking it was a done deal—I was his.

That afternoon, we plunked down $1,500 in half an hour at a baby store. We bought one of everything, including a mega-stroller solid enough for a presidential motorcade. The saleswoman took one look at us and said, "Adopting, huh?"

On the plane to Phoenix, I tried to read Dr. Spock and quit after two pages, not wanting to know how much I didn't know. That would become apparent soon enough. The first bottle I made Nick spilled all over his fancy new Osh Kosh b' Gosh duds. We were too dumb and too scared to know how to put in a nipple. In the airport lounge where I changed my first diaper, I apologized to my son for my ineptitude and asked silently for his forbearance. I was a rookie, an amateur, newer to this game than he was.

People ask all the time whether I'd feel any differently about Nick and Emma if they were my "own" children. I always reply that I can't conceive of it—which is pointed as well as true. It's impossible to imagine loving them more if there were *of* me. I mean, I love their father and the cat and the dog, and we don't share the same DNA.

There is only one sense in which I feel they are not mine—the proprietary one. I do not possess them. Rather I am possessed by them, an irrevocable transaction that occurred the moment our eyes met. There are pictures in our family album of me waiting for Nick, a supplicant reclining in a hotel bed, waiting for my life to change. Then came the knock on the door. And I was down on all fours with him: engaged. I cannot remember getting there. I cannot visualize moving from the unmade bed to the carpeted floor. But in that instant, my posture in life changed forever—from passive to active, from mine to theirs. Sadness was banished. A joyous new fact of life was *a priori* true.

Once you have a child in your arms, you stop thinking about all that went before: the envy, the fear, the humiliations; post-coital tests, injections, inseminations, failures. It's *all* gone. You no longer worry about what it is to be a mother or how to become one because you're too busy *being* one. Your child supplants your pain.

I quit the *Washington Post* where I was a sportswriter, giving up the job of a tomboy's dreams for an imagined life of playing catch in the late afternoon shadows. Who knew a bum shoulder would force me to the sidelines by the time Nick was a year old?

That spring, I took him to opening day at Memorial Stadium in Baltimore. Nick sat on my lap practicing his new word—Eddie! Eddie!—in honor of the Orioles' star

Eddie Murray, while I proudly pointed to the press box where Mommy worked before he came. That it meant nothing to him was irrelevant. He'd put me back in touch with a part of myself that I had locked away in the attic at puberty along with my baseball glove.

And then suddenly he was three and it was time to think about a sibling. That there would be one was a foregone conclusion. Dad's an only child—one of those per household is quite enough. Besides, Nick deserved an ally, someone to share his experience as an adopted child.

Again we had a choice. The adoption agency would have been very happy to find him a brother. Naively, we had believed it was more difficult to adopt boys, assuming that everybody still wants sons. In fact, in the adoption circles, it's a commonly held belief that healthy white females are harder to come by. No one can say precisely why that is or even if it is statistically true. But the woman who placed Emma in my arms explained it this way: It's easier to accept a daughter who fails to meet genetic expectations than a son. Since adopted male children are at greater risk for a variety of dysfunctional behaviors, the argument goes, it is also more likely that they will "fail" in their parents' eyes, a risk not everyone is willing to take.

But for me, a woman whose body language was honed on the ballfield, the far greater risk was that I would fail a girl.

The truth is, I was terrified to have a daughter. I'm not talking about the generic panic newborns inspire with their pink fragility and insatiable needs. I'm talking about the abject fear of being the mother of a female child.

Having a daughter meant answering to my own insecurities about womanliness, self-doubts that preceded infertility but were also reshaped and reawakened by it. It meant consciously choosing to confront the diffuse but intensely intimate concept of femininity. It meant resolving for myself the essential question buried deep within my dysfunctional womb: How much is womanhood defined by biology and specifically by the fact of giving birth?

The social worker arrived for our home study on the appointed day, bringing an application and a whole raft of questions about why we wanted a second child, none of which were anything like my own. What if I get a girl who likes to window shop? Or play with makeup? What if I get a girly-girl? I stared at my much-gnawed nails and had a terrible vision: nail polish.

My pen wavered over the little boxes on the application marked F and M. I told myself: *You don't have to do this.* I reviewed the pros and cons of two little boys. All those hand-me-downs. All that testosterone!

While I was deliberating, Nick arrived in the living room carrying a plastic orange jack-o'-lantern with a wounded baby bird inside. One wing was broken, the other beat frantically against the demented, toothless grin. "Can I keep it, Mom?" he said.

The social worker, no fan of Alfred Hitchcock, cowered in the corner while I appraised the situation: My three-year-old adopted son wanted to adopt a wounded bird that had fallen out of the nest, a baby without a mother. There was no way we were going to keep it. But I could not dismiss his identification with it either—not in front of the social worker in charge of our home study.

Nick handed me his new, feathery friend. I hate birds; I have ever since my mother asphyxiated Chirpie the parakeet with Mr. Clean. It required every bit of courage I could muster not to cut and run. In that moment, with the poor, fuzzy thing beating its one good wing against my chest, I realized that if I could overcome my fear of feathered creatures, I could overcome my fear of having a baby girl too.

I handed the bird back to Nick and told him we'd try to find its mother, hoping the social worker would be impressed by my respect for biological mothers, aviary and otherwise. I started to tell her how often I think about the women who bore my children, always on their birthdays, and always with fondness and gratitude. Sometimes I think I can see them, strong, confident women striding through meadows of wildflowers. But she wasn't interested. She didn't like birds any more than I do.

In a panic, she waved the application in my face. My husband nodded reassuringly. I took up my pen and accepted the challenge. In the end, I couldn't face going through life thinking of myself as too scared of my own femininity to raise a little girl. Six months later, Emma was placed in my arms.

By some act of divine intervention, she arrived on August 24, exactly three years to the day after her brother. She was eight days old and very pink except for her eyes, which were wide-open and as blue as my grandmother's on the day she died. I had the feeling she saw everything, or would soon anyway. I decided I'd better quit biting my nails.

I didn't, of course, but that's the only predictable part of the story. I knew things were going to be different right off because I was worried about what to wear. How do you dress to meet your daughter? I chose pink—OK, dusty rose.

The first thing I did was change her into a hooded gown of bold pink and yellow stripes, an act that made her mine. It was an outfit that said girl but not girly-girl. I promised Emma, as I touched her soft, naked baby skin for the first time, that I would never turn her into a doll, all ribbons and bows.

From the beginning, Emma was a lot more accepting of me than I am of myself. To her I am mother, as much a fait accompli as she is to me. Her unquestioning acceptance of who I am began a long overdue process of reconciliation with myself which continues, under her tutelage, to this day.

I came of age in the last generation to believe that you couldn't play ball with the boys and get asked out too. It never occurred to me that you didn't have to choose between them until one evening a year or so ago when Emma appeared in the front hall wearing her brother's Michael Jordan high tops and unadorned red sweats: no cutesy appliqué, thank you very much. Beneath them, she had on pink tights adorned with gray ballerinas assuming the first position (one of many I never managed). Her earlobes were plastered with four pairs of paste-on earrings, her lips with seventeen different shades of gloss, each perfectly applied. On her hands were her father's thirty-year-old boxing gloves.

"Put 'em up," she said to her brother.

For her, the world isn't either/or. For her, there are no internal contradictions. She doesn't see any reason to choose between the lipstick and the sweats. And now, thanks to her, neither do I.

Soon after the boxing match in the front hall word came home in Emma's backpack about "Being Born Week." I remembered the woman from the adoption agency telling us that the need to see a biological relative and the ability to produce one can be a very tempting combination. Emma's birth mother, who was also adopted, was a teenager when she gave birth. Perhaps getting pregnant gave her a way of feeling close to her biological mother. I was determined that the school officials understand that the stakes in the Tulip Room debate were not academic to me at all.

The morning before the visit of the Pregnant Moms, I stormed the assistant director's office, stomping my feet like some four-year-olds I know. Maybe I was trying to prove that adoptive moms can be equally ferocious in defense of their young. Maybe I was trying to protect myself as much as Emma. At any rate, I was loud.

The administration offered a compromise: A mother of newborn *adopted* twins would bring her babies to visit the class. Everybody would be able to see that adopted newborns looked exactly like any other newborns and adoptive moms look exactly like any other moms.

"Fine," I said. "As long as she's exquisitely happy."

But that evening, the mother of the twins pulled out, having second thoughts about bringing newborns into a classroom full of runny-nosed four-year-olds, adopted babies being every bit as prone to infection as anyone else.

The next morning, just before circle time, the administration capitulated. The assistant director agreed to talk to the kids. I was not invited to come along.

I waited by the phone for a debriefing. This is what I was told. Right off, the head Tulip explained that most kids go home from the hospital with their parents and some go home to their adoptive parents. Not wanting to muddy the waters any further by also explaining *foster* parents, she said that some adopted children go home with *babysitters* before their adoptive families come to get them.

Then it was time for The Moms. The first to speak decided to explain cesarean section, a subject close to her heart and other parts of her anatomy. She even mentioned that some babies "get nicked on the way out." By the time she shut up, the assistant director was lucky to get in a sentence. She said that adopted kids are special because they are chosen.

Then the children were asked for questions or comments. Emma's hand shot up, her pinky finger glittering with a Barbie Band-Aid she'd put on that morning. She had a cut, she explained, which meant she must have been "nicked on the way out." But that was OK because she went home with our babysitter who took good care of her until her dad and I arrived.

My spy in the Tulip Room related the story to me with a straight face, which is more than I can do at this retelling. She said Emma seemed very pleased with herself at having figured it all out. I was left then, as I am now, marveling at the wondrous ability of my daughter to make sense of the folly of adults, especially those, like me, who try so hard to do the right thing.

A tough lesson was learned that day, but not at all the one I expected. I learned that there will be wounding words and unwanted complications, ambiguity and self-doubt, the nicks and cuts of everyday life. No matter how hard I try, ultimately

Emma will have to make sense of them for herself. If she's lucky, she'll have a son or a daughter who'll help her along the way.

My children are my teachers. They have taught me to reject the foolishness of genetic hubris. Because of them, I am a more democratic person. Because they are not *of* me, I do not regard them as tabula rasa on which to inscribe my dreams and expectations. Nick and Emma are the authors of themselves.

Something else: I no longer believe you *become* a mother with a knock on the door, a call in the night, or even seventeen hours of labor. It's an ongoing process. I am always, and still, becoming their mother.

We got out the story I wrote for the Tulip Room the other day. Emma particularly liked the part about coming home on a jet plane and waking her brother up in the middle of the night and going to the beach the next morning with everyone, except the dog who was too loud and not permitted to come.

The picture we sent along with the story was taken on the same beach where we'd picked Nick's name three years before. Emma is lying on her back on a purple blanket, wrapped in a borrowed lime-green afghan, wearing stripes as pink as her cheeks. Her still wrinkled fingers are curled in a fist, except for her pinky, which is pointing at me. I am the unseen person outside the frame, the guiding hand at her side. We are separate, but we are reaching for each other.

Write a letter to your child describing the first moment you saw him or her.

_____

_____

_____

_____

_____

_____

_____

_____

_____

_____

_____

_____

_____

_____

_____

_____

$\mathcal{S}$EE HOW A MOTHER, the best philosopher in practical matters, understands every one of her children and the special differences between them all; and does she not carry herself with true intuition as to their daily needs and with the interpreting philosophy of sensitive love? She is the best trainer of men and has the best mental philosophy, so far as practical things are concerned.

—HENRY WARD BEECHER

BY KATE CHOPIN

MAMZELLE AURÉLIE POSSESSED A GOOD STRONG FIGURE, ruddy cheeks, hair that was changing from brown to gray, and a determined eye. She wore a man's hat about the farm, and an old blue army overcoat when it was cold, and sometimes topboots.

Mamzelle Aurélie had never thought of marrying. She had never been in love. At the age of twenty she had received a proposal, which she had promptly declined, and at the age of fifty she had not yet lived to regret it.

So she was quite alone in the world, except for her dog Ponto, and the workers who lived in her cabins and worked her crops, and the fowls, a few cows, a couple of mules, her gun (with which she shot chicken-hawks), and her religion.

One morning Mamzelle Aurélie stood upon her gallery, contemplating, with arms akimbo, a small band of very small children who, to all intents and purposes, might have fallen from the clouds, so unexpected and bewildering was their coming, and so unwelcome. They were the children of her nearest neighbor, Odile, who was not such a near neighbor, after all.

The young woman had appeared but five minutes before, accompanied by these four children. In her arms she carried little Elodie; she dragged Ti Nomme by an unwilling hand; while Marcéline and Marcélette followed with irresolute steps.

Her face was red and disfigured from tears and excitement. She had been summoned to a neighboring parish by the dangerous illness of her mother; her husband was away in Texas—it seemed to her a million miles away; and Valsin was waiting with the mule-cart to drive her to the station.

"It's no question, Mamzelle Aurélie; you jus' got to keep those youngsters fo' me tell I come back. Dieu sait,'[1] I wouldn' botha you with 'em if it was any otha way to do! Make 'em mine you, Mamzelle Aurélie; don' spare 'em. Me, there, I'm half crazy between the chil'ren, an' Léon not home, an' maybe not even to fine po' maman alive encore!"—a harrowing possibility which drove Odile to take a final hasty and convulsive leave of her disconsolate family.

She left them crowded into the narrow strip of shade on the porch of the long, low house; the white sunlight was beating in on the white old boards; some chickens were scratching in the grass at the foot of the steps, and one had boldly mounted, and

[1] The "Bogeyman."

was stepping heavily, solemnly, and aimlessly across the gallery. There was a pleasant odor of pinks in the air, and the sound of negroes' laughter was coming across the flowering cotton-field.

Mamzelle Aurélie stood contemplating the children. She looked with a critical eye upon Marcéline, who had been left staggering beneath the weight of the chubby Elodie. She surveyed with the same calculating air Marcélette mingling her silent tears with the audible grief and rebellion of Ti Nomme. During those few contemplative moments she was collecting herself, determining upon a line of action which should be identical with a line of duty. She began by feeding them.

If Mamzelle Aurélie's responsibilities might have begun and ended there, they could easily have been dismissed; for her larder was amply provided against an emergency of this nature. But little children are not little pigs; they require and demand attentions which were wholly unexpected by Mamzelle Aurélie, and which she was ill prepared to give.

She was, indeed, very inapt in her management of Odile's children during the first few days. How could she know that Marcélette always wept when spoken to in a loud and commanding tone of voice? It was a peculiarity of Marcélette's. She became acquainted with Ti Nomme's passion for flowers only when he had plucked all the choicest gardenias and pinks for the apparent purpose of critically studying their botanical construction.

" 'Tain't enough to tell 'em, Mamzelle Aurélie," Marcéline instructed her; "you got to tie 'im in a chair. It's w'at maman all time do w'en he's bad: she tie 'im in a

A Mom Is . . . ~ 91

chair." The chair in which Mamzelle Aurélie tied Ti Nomme was roomy and comfortable, and he seized the opportunity to take a nap in it, the afternoon being warm.

At night, when she ordered them one and all to bed as she would have shooed the chickens into the hen-house, they stayed uncomprehending before her. What about the little white nightgowns that had to be taken from the pillow-slip in which they were brought over, and shaken by some strong hand till they snapped like ox-whips? What about the tub of water which had to be brought and set in the middle of the floor, in which the little tired, dusty, sunbrowned feet had every one to be washed sweet and clean? And it made Marcéline and Marcélette laugh merrily—the idea that Mamzelle Aurélie should for a moment have believed that Ti Nomme could fall asleep without being told the story of *Croquemitaine*[2] or *Loupagrou*,[3] or both; or that Elodie could fall asleep at all without being rocked and sung to.

"I tell you, Aunt Ruby," Mamzelle Aurélie informed her cook in confidence; "me, I'd rather manage a dozen plantation' than fo' chil'ren. It's terrassent! Bonté![4] Don't talk to me about chil'ren!"

" 'Tain' ispected sich as you would know airy thing 'bout 'em, Mamzelle Aurélie. I see dat plainly yistiddy w'en I spy dat li'le chile playin' wid yo' baskit o' keys. You don' know dat makes chillun grow up hard-headed, to play wid keys? Des like it make 'em teeth hard to look in a lookin'-glass. Them's the things you got to know in the raisin' an' manigement o' chillun"

[2] The "Bogeyman."
[3] The "Werewolf."
[4] "It's exhausting! Goodness."

Mamzelle Aurélie certainly did not pretend or aspire to such subtle and far-reaching knowledge on the subject as Aunt Ruby possessed, who had "raised five an' bared (buried) six" in her day. She was glad enough to learn a few little mother-tricks to serve the moment's need.

Ti Nomme's sticky fingers compelled her to unearth white aprons that she had not worn for years, and she had to accustom herself to his moist kisses—the expressions of an affectionate and exuberant nature. She got down her sewing-basket, which she seldom used, from the top shelf of the armoire, and placed it within the ready and easy reach which torn slips and buttonless waists demanded. It took her some days to become accustomed to the laughing and crying, the chattering that echoed through the house and around it all day long. And it was not the first or the second night that she could sleep comfortably with little Elodie's hot, plump body pressed close against her, and the little one's warm breath beating her cheek like the fanning of a bird's wing.

But at the end of two weeks Mamzelle Aurélie had grown quite used to these things, and she no longer complained.

It was also at the end of two weeks that Mamzelle Aurélie, one evening, looking away toward the crib where the cattle were being fed, saw Valsin's blue cart turning the bend of the road. Odile sat beside the mulatto, upright and alert. As they drew near, the young woman's beaming face indicated that her homecoming was a happy one.

But this coming, unannounced and unexpected, threw Mamzelle Aurélie into a flutter that was almost agitation. The children had to be gathered. Where was Ti

Nomme? Yonder in the shed, putting an edge on his knife at the grindstone. And Marcéline and Marcélette? Cutting and fashioning doll-rags in the corner of the gallery. As for Elodie, she was safe enough in Mamzelle Aurélie's arms; and she had screamed with delight at sight of the familiar blue cart which was bringing her mother back to her.

The excitement was all over, and they were gone. How still it was when they were gone! Mamzelle Aurélie stood upon the gallery, looking and listening. She could no longer see the cart; the red sunset and the blue-gray twilight had together flung a purple mist across the fields and road that hid it from her view. She could no longer hear the wheezing and creaking of its wheels. But she could still faintly hear the shrill, glad voices of the children.

She turned into the house. There was much work awaiting her, for the children had left a sad disorder behind them; but she did not at once set about the task of righting it. Mamzelle Aurélie seated herself beside the table. She gave one slow glance through the room, into which the evening shadows were creeping and deepening around her solitary figure. She let her head fall down upon her bended arm, and began to cry. Oh, but she cried! Not softly, as women often do. She cried like a man, with sobs that seemed to tear her very soul. She did not notice Ponto licking her hand.

My Bondage and My Freedom

BY FREDERICK DOUGLASS

MY MOTHER WAS HIRED OUT TO A MR. STEWART, who lived about twelve miles from old master's, and, being a field hand, she seldom had leisure, by day, for the performance of the journey. The nights and the distance were both obstacles to her visits. She was obliged to walk. . . . It was a greater luxury than slavery could afford, to allow a black slave-mother a horse or a mule, upon which to travel twenty-four miles, when she could walk the distance. Besides, it is deemed a foolish whim for a slave-mother to manifest concern to see her children, and, in one point of view, the case is made out—she can do nothing for them. She has no control over them; the master is even more than the mother, in all matters touching the fate of her child. Why, then, should she give herself any concern? She has no responsibility. Such is the reasoning, and such the practice. The iron rule of the plantation, always passionately and violently enforced in that neighborhood, makes flogging the penalty of failing to be in the field before sunrise in the morning, unless special permission be given to the absenting slave. "I went to see my child," is no excuse to the ear or heart of the overseer.

One of the visits of my mother to me, while at Col. Lloyd's, I remember very vividly, as affording a bright gleam of a mother's love, and the earnestness of a mother's care.

I had on that day offended "Aunt Katy" (called "Aunt" by way of respect), the cook of old master's establishment. I do not now remember the nature of my offense in this instance, for my offenses were numerous in that quarter, greatly depending, however, upon the mood of Aunt Katy, as to their heinousness; but she had adopted, that day, her favorite mode of punishing me, namely, making me go without food all day—that is, from after breakfast. The first hour or two after dinner, I succeeded pretty well in keeping up my spirits; but though I made an excellent stand against the foe, and fought bravely during the afternoon, I knew I must be conquered at last, unless I got the accustomed reenforcement of a slice of corn bread, at sundown. Sundown came, but *no bread*, and in its stead, there came the threat, with a scowl well suited to its terrible import, that she "meant to *starve the life out of me*!" Brandishing her knife, she chopped off the heavy slices for the other children, and put the loaf away, muttering, all the while, her savage designs upon myself. Against this disappointment, for I was expecting that her heart would relent at last, I made an extra effort to maintain my dignity; but when I saw all the other children around me with merry and satisfied faces, I could stand it no longer. I went out behind the house, and cried like a fine fellow! When tired of this, I returned to the kitchen, sat by the fire, and brooded over my hard lot. I was too hungry to sleep. While I sat in the corner, I caught sight of an ear of Indian corn on an upper shelf of the kitchen. I watched my chance, and got it, and, shelling off a few grains, I put it back again. The grains in my hand, I quickly put in some ashes, and covered them with embers, to roast them. All this I did at the risk of getting a brutal thumping, for Aunt Katy could beat, as well as starve me. My corn was not long in roasting, and, with my keen appetite, it did not matter even if the grains were not exactly done. I eagerly pulled them out, and placed them on my stool, in a clever little pile. Just as I began to help myself to my very dry meal, in came my dear mother. And now, dear reader, a scene occurred which was altogether worth beholding, and to me it was instructive as well as interesting. The friendless and hungry boy, in his extremest need—and when he did not dare to look for succor—found himself in the strong, protecting arms of a mother; a mother who was, at the moment (being endowed with high powers of manner as well as matter) more than a match for all his enemies. I shall never forget the indescribable expression of her countenance, when I told her that I had had no food since morning; and that Aunt Katy said she "meant to starve the life out of me." There was pity in her glance at me, and a fiery indignation at Aunt Katy at the same time; and, while she took the corn from me, and gave me a large ginger cake, in its stead, she read Aunt Katy a lecture which she never forgot. My mother threatened her with complaining to old master in my behalf; for the latter, though harsh and cruel himself, at times, did not sanction the meanness, injustice, partiality and oppressions enacted by Aunt Katy in the kitchen. That night I learned the fact that I was not only a child, but somebody's child. The "sweet cake" my mother gave me was in the shape of a heart, with a rich, dark ring glazed upon the edge of it. I was victorious, and well off for the moment; prouder, on my mother's knee, than a king upon his throne. But my triumph was short. I dropped off to sleep, and waked in the morning only to find my mother gone, and myself left at the mercy of the sable virago, dominant in my old master's kitchen, whose fiery wrath was my constant dread. I do not remember to have seen my mother after this occurrence.

Working mother is a misnomer. . . .
It implies that any mother without
a definite career is indolently not working,
lolling around eating bon-bons, reading
novels, and watching soap operas.
But the word "mother" is already
a synonym for some of the hardest,
most demanding work ever shouldered
by any human. —LIZ SMITH

Mother's Apron

BY MARJORIE HOLMES

THERE WAS A GOOD EXCUSE FOR APRONS IN OUR MOTHERS' DAY. In that blissful pre-cholesterol era, hardly anybody broiled or pressure-cooked; no, foods were fried lengthily, smokily, often sputteringly, in good old-fashioned lard.

To bake a cake, you didn't simply open a package and make a few absentminded gestures with an electric mixer. You coped long and lovingly with flour and eggs and maybe clabbered milk, pausing for good measure to shake down the ashes in the old coal range, smash more kindling across your knees, and shovel in more cobs or chunks of rich, black, dusty coal. An apron was not only part of a woman's uniform of domesticity; it was protection.

Mothers continued to prepare for their day's assault upon the premises by donning layer upon layer of garments, culminating with a "housedress." A "housedress"

might be vaguely pretty, with a bow or a few buttons on it, but mostly it was plain, functional, and washable, with all elements of character or imagination reduced to the absolute minimum.

The costume was then crowned with a dustcap. The cap was often plain sturdy gingham to match the dress. Or it might be a perky concoction of lace and ribbon rosettes. In any case, it served the purpose of protecting the hair from the dust that mothers whacked or shook or swept from the house.

And always, as a kind of extra fortification from all this, a mother wore an apron. She put it on over her housedress in the morning, and she didn't remove it until she cleaned up for the afternoon. Then, like as not, she donned a fresh one from her ample stock.

Women were better organized then, perhaps because they had to be. They seldom had a car in the driveway to whisk them off to meetings or the supermarket while the clothes washed and dried. My mother certainly never did the impulse cleaning to which I'm prone, nor popped a pie in the oven or started ironing after dark. As with her neighbors, each day was sacred to its appointed tasks—the laundry, the baking, the scrubbing; what's more, she rose early, accomplished the scheduled undertaking, and was ready for the sacred rite of making herself presentable by two o'clock. (To be "caught dirty" any time after three would have been sheer disgrace.)

This involved at least a sponge bath with a kettle of cistern water heated on the stove, the neat doing-up of hair with a number of pins and tortoiseshell combs, putting on a "good" dress as opposed to a housedress, and silk instead of cotton stockings, finishing off with a touch of rice powder and a dab of cologne. She was then ready for any callers who might drop in; or she'd lie down with the latest installment of a Kathleen Norris serial.

This brief span during the afternoon was the only time she was minus an apron. And when she arose to start supper, did she change, as we are wont to, into something comfortable if sloppy? No, indeed, she simply protected her daintiness with a nice fresh apron. Sometimes a big apron that encircled her neck like loving arms; sometimes one that tied at the waist in a bow that brothers or your dad would yank when they wanted to tease her. If company was coming, it would be a fancy apron, all organdy frills, the kind women still wear for serving dinners and sociables at the church. But family apron or company apron, it was always crisp and pretty and clean, and she often wore it to the table.

Frequently she continued to wear it on into the evening after the dishes were done. Standing at the back fence visiting with a neighbor, strolling about the yard to see about her flowers, or sitting on the porch in the twilight watching the children playing redlight or catching fireflies in a jar. And if the air were chilly, she wrapped her arms in her apron to keep them warm.

An apron was a part of Mother—like her laugh or her eyes or her big black pocketbook. And it was more than her protection against the hazards of cooking and keeping house—it was a kind of protection for you as well. It was big enough to shelter you too sometimes if you were cold. There was always a handkerchief for you in one of its roomy pockets. It was a part of her lap.

And her apron gave you assurance. Rushing in from school or play, even if you didn't see or hear her, you felt better just finding that apron hanging behind the kitchen door or dangling across a chair. Her apron, smelling of cookies and starch and Mother. It comforted you. It made you feel secure.

Maybe that's why our youngsters instinctively want us to own aprons. Lots of aprons. And to wear one now and then. Why we ourselves can't resist buying them at bazaars. Maybe we still feel the strong, sweet tug of apron strings. We remember the time when an apron meant a lap to be cuddled on, a pocket with a hanky to wipe your nose on, someone who cared about you. The days when a mother's apron symbolized love!

$\mathscr{W}$HO TAUGHT ME PATIENCE, if not you? The sometimes-consoling rituals of housekeeping, small simple finite tasks executed with love or at any rate bemused affection, cheerful resignation. You tried to teach me to knit, and to sew, for which feminine activities I demonstrated little talent if, at the outset, energy and hope. You had more success teaching me to iron, a dreamy mesmerizing task I seem to have liked, as girls will, in small intermittent doses.

—**JOYCE CAROL OATES,**
in a letter to her mother on her mother's 78th birthday

I WAS AN APT STUDENT AT SCHOOL and before I was eighteen I had earned a teacher's certificate of the second grade and would gladly have remained in school a few more years, but I had, unwittingly, agreed to marry the man who is now my husband, and tho I begged to be released, his will was so much the stronger that I was unable to free myself without wounding a loving heart, and could not find it in my heart to do so. . . .

I always had a passion for reading; during girlhood it was along educational lines; in young womanhood it was for love stories, which remained ungratified because my father thought it sinful to read stories of any kind, and especially love stories.

Later, when I was married, I borrowed everything I could find in the line of novels and stories, and read them by stealth still, for my husband thought it a willful waste of time to read anything and that it showed a lack of love for him if I would rather read than to talk to him when I had a few moments of leisure, and, in order to avoid giving offense and still gratify my desire, I would only read when he was not at the house, thereby greatly curtailing my already too limited reading hours. . . .

It is only during the last three years that I have had the news to read, for my husband is so very penurious that he would never consent to subscribing for papers of any kind and that old habit of avoiding that which would give offense was so fixed that I did not dare to break it.

The addition of two children to our family never altered or interfered with the established order of things to any appreciable extent. My strenuous outdoor life agreed with me, and even when my children were born I was splendidly prepared for the ordeal and made rapid recovery. . . .

Any bright morning in the latter part of May I am out of bed at four o'clock; next, after I have dressed and combed my hair, I start a fire in the kitchen stove, . . . sweep the floors and then cook breakfast.

While the other members of the family are eating breakfast I strain away the morning's milk (for my husband milks the cows while I get breakfast), and fill my husband's dinnerpail, for he will go to work on our other farm for the day.

By this time it is half-past five o'clock, my husband is gone to his work, and the stock loudly pleading to be turned into the pastures. The younger cattle, a half-dozen steers, are left in the pasture at night, and I now drive the two cows a half-quarter mile and turn them in with the others, come back, and then there's a horse in the barn

that belongs in a field where there is no water, which I take to a spring quite a distance from the barn; bring it back and turn it into a field with the sheep, a dozen in number, which are housed at night.

The young calves are then turned out into the warm sunshine, and the stock hogs, which are kept in a pen, are clamoring for feed, and I carry a pailful of swill to them, and hasten to the house and turn out the chickens and put out feed and water for them, and it is, perhaps, 6:30 a.m.

I have not eaten breakfast yet, but that can wait; I make the beds next and straighten things up in the living room, for I dislike to have the early morning caller find my house topsy-turvy. When this is done I go to the kitchen, which also serves as a dining room, and uncover the table, and take a mouthful of food occasionally as I pass to and fro at my work until my appetite is appeased.

By the time the work is done in the kitchen it is about 7:15 a.m., and the cool morning hours have flown, and no hoeing done in the garden yet, and the children's toilet has to be attended to and churning has to be done.

Finally the children are washed and churning done, and it is eight o'clock, and the sun getting hot, but no matter, weeds die quickly when cut down in the heat of the day, and I use the hoe to a good advantage until the dinner hour, which is 11:30 a.m. We come in, and I comb my hair, and put fresh flowers in it, and eat a cold dinner, put out feed and water for the chickens; set a hen, perhaps, sweep the floors again; sit down and rest and read a few moments, and it is nearly one o'clock, and I sweep the door yard while I am waiting for the clock to strike the hour.

I make and sow a flower bed, dig around some shrubbery, and go back to the garden to hoe until time to do the chores at night. . . .

I hoe in the garden till four o'clock; then I go into the house and get supper . . . when supper is all ready it is set aside, and I pull a few hundred plants of tomato, sweet potato or cabbage for transplanting . . . I then go after the horse, water him, and put him in the barn; call the sheep and house them, and go after the cows and milk them, feed the hogs, put down hay for three horses, and put oats and corn in their troughs, and set those plants and come in and fasten up the chickens. . . . It is 8 o'clock p.m.; my husband has come home, and we are eating supper; when we are through eating I make the beds ready, and the children and their father go to bed, and I wash the dishes and get things in shape to get breakfast quickly next morning. . . .

All the time that I have been going about this work I have been thinking of things I have read . . . and of other things which I have a desire to read, but cannot hope to while the present condition exists.

As a natural consequence there are daily, numerous instances of absentmindedness on my part; many things left undone. . . . My husband never fails to remind me that it is caused by my reading so much; that I would get along much better if I should never see a book or paper. . . .

I use an old fashioned churn, and the process of churning occupies from thirty minutes to three hours, according to the condition of the cream, and I always read something while churning. . . .

—ANONYMOUS (LATE 19TH CENTURY)

Where there is
a mother in the house,
matters speed well.

—AMOS BRONSON ALCOTT

The Song of the Old Mother

I rise in the dawn, and I kneel and blow
Till the seed of the fire flicker and glow.
And then I must scrub, and bake, and sweep,
Till stars are beginning to blink and peep;
But the young lie long and dream in their bed
Of the matching of ribbons, the blue and the red,
And their day goes over in idleness,
And they sigh if the wind but lift up a tress.
Wile I must work, because I am old
And the seed of the fire gets feeble and cold.

—WILLIAM BUTLER YEATS

EXCERPT FROM
A Song for Mary

BY DENNIS SMITH

MY EARLIEST MEMORY is of my mother taking in a big pile of shirts from a neighbor down the hall on 56th Street.

"Work," she said, plopping the shirts into the kitchen bathtub, "is the thing that supports the neck."

It was a long time before I knew what she was talking about, and it might be her greatest lesson. Whether it is ironing shirts or being a firefighter, twenty-year pension or not, caring about your work is the thing that supports the neck in keeping the head high.

If there is anyone to thank for getting me through to where I am, it is my mother. She is having a tough time with the stairs now, and I know that she will have to move from the tenement on 54th Street pretty soon, by the time she retires from the telephone company, anyway.

I try to see her once a week. She comes to our house mostly, to see the kids, to baby-sit while Pat and I go out to a movie.

I wish she would stop smoking. If she stopped smoking, she could do another few years of climbing the stairs. But she has been combing her hair one way for most of her life, and I know that she would not take the advice she once gave me to use a brush.

"I'm going to have to put a carton of Old Golds in your coffin the day they bury you, Mom," I said to her recently, when we were sitting across from each other, having a cup of coffee.

"Don't forget the matches," she returned quickly, with a wink of her eye.

I like being with my mother. She has humor. She might have some prejudices and periods of short temper also, but they are a consequence of a longtime loneliness, I think, and a small price to pay for giving up any chance of a normal social life to care for her two sons.

I believe she has earned the right to tons of happiness, but it doesn't look like much will come her way. I suppose she is like a million other women who were left alone with a few kids by a husband who became absent for whatever reason. They are like the fifth estate in America, and what they do is every bit as consequential for America's future as anything that gets written in a newspaper or done in Congress, a church, or a synagogue.

I am sure it is not easy to be alone now, but my mother does it with her chin held high, anyway. She works six days a week at the telephone company. She comes home after work, makes a small dinner, gets into bed, reads the *Daily News*, and sips a small glass of port. She does this every night without fail.

It may not be much of a life, but it's a respectable one, I think. I make sure I call her every day, to let her know that she is being thought of, to thank her in my own way.

My earliest memory of my mother is . . .

_____

_____

_____

_____

_____

_____

_____

_____

_____

_____

_____

_____

_____

_____

To Mother

I hope that soon, dear Mother,
You and I may be
In the quiet room my fancy
Has so often made for thee—

The pleasant, sunny chamber;
The cushioned easy-chair;
The book laid for your reading;
The vase of flowers fair;

The desk beside the window
Where the sun shines warm
 and bright,
And there in ease and quiet
The promised book you write,

While I sit close beside you,
Content at last to see
That you can rest, dear Mother,
And I can cherish thee.

—LOUISA MAY ALCOTT

Rock Me To Sleep

Backward, turn backward, O Time, in your flight,
Make me a child again just for to-night!
Mother, come back from the echoless shore,
Take me again to your heart as of yore;
Kiss from my forehead the furrows of care,
Smooth the few silver threads out of my hair.
Over my slumbers your loving watch keep
Rock me to sleep, mother, —rock me to sleep.

Backward, flow backward, O Tide of the years;
I am so weary of toil and of tears,
Toil without recompense, tears all in vain,
Take them, and give me my childhood again;
I have grown weary of dust and decay,
Weary of flinging my soul-wealth away;
Weary of sowing for others to reap,
Rock me to sleep, mother, —rock me to sleep.

Tired of the hollow, the base, the untrue,
Mother, oh mother, my heart calls for you!
Many a summer the grass has grown green,
Blossomed and faded, our faces between.
Yet, with strong yearning and passionate pain,
Long I to-night for your presence again,
Come from the silence so long and so deep;
Rock me to sleep, mother, —rock me to sleep.

Over my heart, in the days that are flown,
No love like mother-love ever has shone;
No other worship abides and endures,
Faithful, unselfish, and patient like yours;
None like a mother can charm away pain,
From the sick soul and the world-weary brain.
Slumber's soft calms o'er my heavy lids creep,
Rock me to sleep, mother, —rock me to sleep.

Come let your brown hair, just lighted with gold,
Fall on your shoulders again as of old;
Let it drop over my forehead to-night,
Shading my faint eyes away from the light;
For with its sunny-edged shadows once more
Happily will throng the sweet vision of yore;
Lovingly, softly, its bright billows sweep;
Rock me to sleep, mother, —rock me to sleep.

Mother, dear mother, the years have been long
Since I last listened to your lullaby song;
Sing, then, and unto my soul it shall seem
Womanhood's years have been only a dream,
Clasped to your heart in a loving embrace
With your light lashes just sweeping my face,
Never hereafter to wake or to weep;
Rock me to sleep, mother, —rock me to sleep.

—ELIZABETH AKERS ALLEN

PART II:

Mother's Helper

Baby, baby, ope your eye,
For the sun is in the sky,
And he's peeping once again
Through the frosty window pane;
Little baby, do not keep
Any longer fast asleep.

There, now, sit in mother's lap,
That she may untie your cap,
For the little strings have got
Twisted into such a knot;
Ah! for shame, —you've been
   at play
With the bobbin, as you lay.

There it comes, —now let me see
Where your petticoats can be;
Oh, —they're in the window seat,
Folded very smooth and neat:
When my baby older grows
She shall double up her clothes.

Now one pretty little kiss,
For dressing you as neat as this,
And before we go downstairs,
Don't forget to say your pray'rs,
For 't is God who loves to keep
Little babies in their sleep.

—JANE TAYLOR

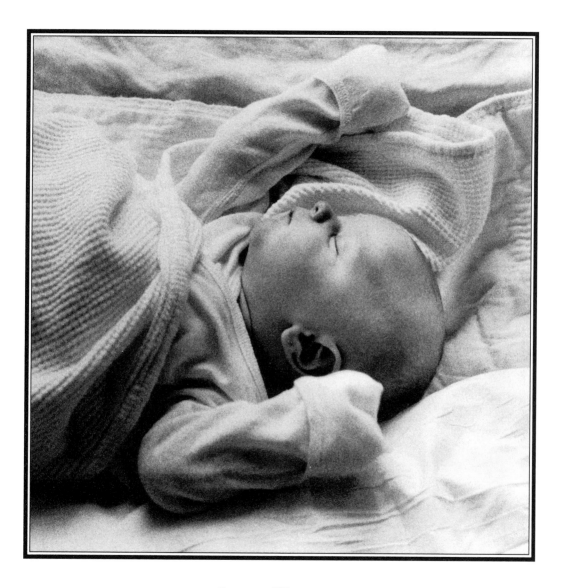

Twinkle, Twinkle, Little Star

Twinkle, twinkle, little star,
How I wonder what you are,
Up above the world so high,
Like a diamond in the sky.
 Twinkle, twinkle, little star,
 How I wonder what you are.

When the blazing sun is gone,
When it nothing shines upon,
Then you show your little light,
Twinkle, twinkle all the night.
 Twinkle, twinkle, little star,
 How I wonder what you are.

Then the traveler in the dark
Thanks you for your tiny spark.
Could he see which way to go
If you did not twinkle so?
  Twinkle, twinkle, little star,
    How I wonder what you are.

In the dark blue sky you keep,
While you through my curtains peep,
And you never shut your eye
Till the sun is in the sky.
  Twinkle, twinkle, little star,
    How I wonder what you are.

Cinderella
OR THE LITTLE GLASS SLIPPER

BY CHARLES PERRAULT

ONCE THERE WAS A GENTLEMAN WHO MARRIED, for his second wife, the proudest and most haughty woman that was ever seen. She had, by a former husband, two daughters of her own humour, who were, indeed, exactly like her in all things. He had likewise, by another wife, a young daughter, but of unparalleled goodness and sweetness of temper, which she took from her mother, who was the best creature in the world.

No sooner were the ceremonies of the wedding over but the mother-in-law began to show herself in her true colours. She could not bear the good qualities of this pretty girl, and the less because they made her own daughters appear the more odious. She employed her in the meanest work of the house: she scoured the dishes, tables, etc., and rubbed madam's chamber, and those of misses, her daughters; she lay up in a sorry garret, upon a wretched straw bed, while her sisters lay in fine rooms, with floors all inlaid, upon beds of the very newest fashion, and where they had looking-glasses so large that they might see themselves at their full length from head to foot.

The poor girl bore all patiently, and dared not tell her father, who would have rattled her off; for his wife governed him entirely. When she had done her work, she used to go into the chimney-corner, and sit down among cinders and ashes, which made her commonly be called Cinderwench; but the youngest, who was not so rude and uncivil as the eldest, called her Cinderella. However, Cinderella, notwithstanding her mean apparel, was a hundred times handsomer than her sisters, though they were always dressed very richly.

It happened that the King's son gave a ball, and invited all persons of fashion to it. Our young misses were also invited, for they cut a very grand figure among the quality. They were mightily delighted at this invitation, and wonderfully busy in choosing out such gowns, petticoats, and head-clothes as might become them. This was a new trouble to Cinderella; for it was she who ironed her sister's linen, and plaited their ruffles; they talked all day long of nothing but how they should be dressed.

"For my part," said the eldest, "I will wear my red velvet suit with French trimming."

"And I," said the youngest, "shall have my usual petticoat; but then, to make amends for that, I will put on my gold-flowered manteau, and my diamond stomacher, which is far from being the most ordinary one in the world."

They sent for the best tire-woman they could get to make up their head-dresses and adjust their double pinners, and they had their red brushes and patches from Mademoiselle de la Poche.

Cinderella was likewise called up to them to be consulted in all these matters, for she had excellent notions, and advised them always for the best, nay, and offered her services to dress their heads, which they were very willing she should do. As she was doing this, they said to her:

"Cinderella, would you not be glad to go to the ball?"

"Alas!" said she, "you only jeer me; it is not for such as I am to go thither."

"Thou art in the right of it," replied they; "it would make the people laugh to see a Cinderwench at a ball."

Anyone but Cinderella would have dressed their heads awry, but she was very good, and dressed them perfectly well. They were almost two days without eating, so much they were transported with joy. They broke above a dozen of laces in trying to be laced up close, that they might have a fine slender shape, and they were continually at their looking-glass. At last the happy day came; they went to Court, and Cinderella followed them with her eyes as long as she could, and when she had lost sight of them, she fell a-crying.

Her godmother, who saw her all in tears, asked her what was the matter.

"I wish I could—I wish I could—;" she was not able to speak the rest, being interrupted by her tears and sobbing.

This godmother of hers, who was a fairy, said to her, "Thou wishes thou couldst go to the ball; is it not so?"

"Y—es," cried Cinderella, with a great sight.

"Well," said her godmother, "be but a good girl, and I will contrive that thou shalt go." Then she took her into her chamber, and said to her, "Run into the garden, and bring me a pumpkin."

Cinderella went immediately to gather the finest she could get, and brought it to her godmother, not being able to imagine how this pumpkin could make her go to the ball. Her godmother scooped out all the inside of it, having left nothing but the rind; which done, she struck it with her wand, and the pumpkin was instantly turned into a fine coach, gilded all over with gold.

She then went to look into her mouse-trap, where she found six mice, all alive, and ordered Cinderella to lift up a little the trapdoor, when, giving each mouse, as it went out, a little tap with her wand, the mouse was that moment turned into a fine horse, which altogether made a very fine set of six horses of a beautiful mouse-colored dapple-grey. Being at a loss for a coachman, "I will go and see," says Cinderella, "if there is never a rat in the rat-trap—we may make a coachman of him."

"Thou art in the right," replied her godmother; "go and look."

Cinderella brought the trap to her, and in it there were three huge rats. The fairy made choice of one of the three which had the largest beard, and, having touched him with her wand, he was turned into a fat, jolly coachman, who had the smartest whiskers eyes ever beheld. After that, she said to her:

"Go again into the garden, and you will find six lizards behind the watering-pot, bring them to me."

She had no sooner done so but her godmother turned them into six footmen, who skipped up immediately behind the coach, with their liveries all bedaubed with gold and silver, and clung as close behind each other as if they had done nothing else their whole lives. The Fairy then said to Cinderella:

"Well, you see here an equipage fit to go to the ball with; are you not pleased with it?"

"Oh! yes," cried she; "but must I go thither as I am, in these nasty rags?"

Her godmother only just touched her with her wand, and, at the same instant, her clothes were turned into cloth of gold and silver, all beset with jewels. This done, she gave her a pair of glass slippers, the prettiest in the whole world. Being thus decked out, she got up into her coach; but her godmother, above all things, commanded her not to stay till after midnight, telling her, at the same time, that if she stayed one moment longer, the coach would be a pumpkin again, her horses mice, her coachman a rat, her footmen lizards, and her clothes become just as they were before.

She promised her godmother she would not fail of leaving the ball before midnight; and then away she drives, scarce able to contain herself for joy. The King's son, who was told that a great princess, whom nobody knew, was come, ran out to receive her; he gave her his hand as she alighted out of the coach, and led her into the hall, among all the company. There was immediately a profound silence, they left off dancing, and the violins ceased to play, so attentive was everyone to contemplate the singular beauties of the unknown new-comer. Nothing was then heard but a confused noise of:

"Ha! how handsome she is! Ha! how handsome she is!"

The King himself, old as he was, could not help watching her, and telling the Queen softly that it was a long time since he had seen so beautiful and lovely a creature.

All the ladies were busied in considering her clothes and headdress, that they might have some made next day after the same pattern, provided they could meet with such fine materials and as able hands to make them.

The King's son conducted her to the most honourable seat, and afterwards took her out to dance with him; she danced so very gracefully that they all more and more admired her. A fine collation was served up, whereof the young prince ate not a morsel, so intently was he busied in gazing on her.

She went and sat down by her sisters, showing them a thousand civilities, giving them part of the oranges and citrons which the Prince had presented her with, which very much surprised them, for they did not know her. While Cinderella was thus amusing her sisters, she heard the clock strike eleven and three-quarters, whereupon she immediately made a courtesy to the company and hasted away as fast as she could.

Being got home, she ran to seek out her godmother, and, after having thanked her, she said she could not but heartily wish she might go next day to the ball, because the King's son had desired her.

As she was eagerly telling her godmother whatever had passed at the ball, her two sisters knocked at the door, which Cinderella ran and opened.

"How long you have stayed!" cried she, gaping, rubbing her eyes and stretching herself as if she had been just waked out of her sleep; she had not, however, any manner of inclination to sleep since they went from home.

"If thou hadst been at the ball," says one of her sisters, "thou wouldst not have been tired with it. There came thither the finest princess, the most beautiful ever was seen with mortal eyes; she showed us a thousand civilities, and gave us oranges and citrons."

Cinderella seemed very indifferent in the matter; indeed, she asked them the name of that princess; but they told her they did not know it, and that the King's son was very uneasy on her account and would give all the world to know who she was. At this Cinderella, smiling, replied:

"She must, then, be very beautiful indeed; how happy you have been! Could not I see her? Ah! dear Miss Charlotte, do lend me your yellow suit of clothes which you wear every day."

"Ay, to be sure!" cried Miss Charlotte: "lend my clothes to such a dirty Cinderwench as thou art! I should be a fool."

Cinderella, indeed, expected well such answer, and was very glad of the refusal; for she would have been sadly put to it if her sister had lent her what she asked for jestingly.

The next day the two sisters were at the ball, and so was Cinderella, but dressed more magnificently than before. The King's son was always by her, and never ceased his compliments and kind speeches to her; to whom all this was so far from being tiresome that she quite forgot what her godmother had recommended to her; so that she, at last, counted the clock striking twelve when she took it to be no more than eleven; she then rose up and fled, as nimble as a deer. The Prince followed, but could not overtake her. She left behind one of her glass slippers, which the Prince took up most carefully. She got home, but quite out of breath, and in her nasty old clothes, having nothing left her of all her finery but one of the little slippers, fellow to that she dropped. The guards at the palace gate were asked:

If they had not see a princess go out.

Who said: They had seen nobody go out but a young girl, very meanly dressed, and who had more the air of a poor country wench than a gentlewoman.

When the two sisters returned from the ball Cinderella asked them: If they had been well diverted, and if the fine lady had been there.

They told her: Yes, but that she hurried away immediately when it struck twelve, and with so much haste that she dropped one of her little glass slippers, the prettiest in the world, which the King's son had taken up; that he had done nothing but look at her all the time at the ball, and that most certainly he was very much in love with the beautiful person who owned the glass slipper.

What they said was very true; for a few days after the King's son caused it to be proclaimed, by sound of trumpet, that he would marry her whose foot this slipper would just fit. They whom he employed began to try it upon the princesses, then the duchesses and all the Court, but in vain; it was brought to the two sisters, who did all they possibly could to thrust their foot into the slipper, but they could not effect it. Cinderella, who saw all this, and knew her slipper, said to them, laughing:

"Let me see if it will not fit me."

Her sisters burst out a-laughing, and began to banter her. The gentleman who was sent to try the slipper looked earnestly at Cinderella, and, finding her very handsome, said:

It was but just that she should try, and that he had orders to let everyone make trial.

He obliged Cinderella to sit down, and, putting the slipper to her foot, he found it went on very easily, and fitted her as if it had been made of wax. The astonishment her two sisters were in was excessively great, but still abundantly greater when Cinderella pulled out of her pocket the other slipper, and put it on her foot. Thereupon, in came her godmother, who, having touched with her wand Cinderella's clothes, made them richer and more magnificent than any of those she had before.

And now her two sisters found her to be that fine, beautiful lady whom they had seen at the ball. They threw themselves at her feet to beg pardon for all the ill-treatment they had made her undergo. Cinderella took them up, and, as she embraced them, cried:

That she forgave them with all her heart, and desired them always to love her.

She was conducted to the young Prince, dressed as she was; he thought her more charming than ever, and, a few days after, married her. Cinderella, who was no less good than beautiful, gave her two sisters lodgings in the palace, and that very same day matched them with two great lords of the Court.

Humpty Dumpty

Humpty Dumpty sat on a wall,
Humpty Dumpty had a great fall;
All the King's horses and all the King's men
Couldn't put Humpty together again.

Hey! Diddle Diddle

Hey! diddle diddle,

the cat and the fiddle,

The cow jump'd over the moon.

The little dog laugh'd to see such sport,

And the dish ran after the spoon.

The Emperor's New Clothes

BY HANS CHRISTIAN ANDERSEN

MANY YEARS AGO THERE LIVED AN EMPEROR who was so fond of new clothes that he spent all his money on them. He did not care about his soldiers, he did not care about the theater; he only liked to go out walking to show off his new clothes. He had a coat for every hour of the day; and just as they say of a king, "He is in the council chamber," they always said here, "The emperor is in the wardrobe."

In the great city in which the emperor lived there was always something going on; every day many strangers came there. One day two impostors arrived who announced they were weavers, and said they knew how to manufacture the most beautiful cloth imaginable. Not only were the texture and pattern uncommonly beautiful, but the clothes which were made of the stuff possessed this wonderful property, they were

invisible to anyone who was not fit for his office or who was unpardonably stupid.

"My, oh, my," said the people. "Think of that!"

"Those must indeed be splendid clothes," said the emperor to himself. "If I had them on I could find out which men in my kingdom are unfit for the offices they hold; I could distinguish the wise from the stupid! Yes, this cloth must be woven for me at once."

And he gave both the impostors money that they might begin their work.

They placed two weaving looms and pretended they were working, but they had not the least thing on them. They also demanded the finest silk and the best gold, which they put in their pockets, and worked at the empty looms till late into the night.

I should like very much to know how much they have woven, thought the emperor. But he remembered, when he thought about it, that whoever was stupid or not fit for his office would not be able to see it. Now he certainly believed that he had nothing to fear for himself, but he wanted first to send somebody else in order to see how he stood with regard to his office. Everybody in the whole town knew what a wonderful power the cloth had, and all were curious to see how bad or how stupid their neighbor was.

"I will send my old and honored minister to the weavers," said the emperor. "He can judge best what the cloth is like, for he has intellect, and no one understands his office better than he."

Now the good old minister went into the hall where the two imposters sat working at the empty looms.

Dear me! thought he, opening his eyes wide. I can see nothing! But he did not say so.

Both the impostors begged him to be so kind as to step closer, and asked him if it were not of beautiful texture and lovely colors. They pointed to the empty loom, and the poor old minister went forward rubbing his eyes. But he could see nothing, for there was nothing there.

"Dear, dear," he said to himself, "can I be stupid? I have never thought that, and nobody must know it! Can I be unfit for my office? No, I must certainly not say I cannot see the cloth!"

"Have you nothing to say about it?" asked one of the men who was weaving.

"Oh, it is lovely, most lovely!" answered the old minister, looking through his spectacles. "What a texture! What colors! Yes, I will certainly tell the emperor that it pleases me very much."

"Now we are delighted to hear that," said both the weavers, and thereupon they named the colors and explained the making of the pattern.

The old minister paid great attention so he could tell it all to the emperor when he came back to him, which he did.

The impostors now wanted more money, more silk and more gold to use in their weaving. They put it all in their own pockets, and there were no threads on the looms but they went on as they had before, working at the empty looms. The emperor soon sent another worthy statesman to see how the weaving was progressing and whether the cloth would soon be finished. It was the same with him as with the first one; he looked and looked, but because there was nothing on the empty looms he could see nothing.

"Is it not a beautiful piece of cloth?" asked the two impostors, as they described the splendid material which was not there.

Stupid I am not, thought the man, so it must be my good office for which I am not fitted. It is strange, certainly, but no one must be allowed to notice it. And so he praised the cloth which he did not see, and expressed his delight at the beautiful colors and the splendid texture.

"Yes, it is quite beautiful," he said to the emperor.

Everybody in the town was talking of the magnificent cloth.

Now the emperor wanted to see it himself while it was still on the loom. With a great crowd of select followers, among whom were both the worthy statesmen who had already been there before, he went to the cunning imposters, who were now weaving with all their might, but without fiber or thread, of course.

"Is it not splendid!" said both the old statesmen who had already been there. "See, Your Majesty, what a texture! What colors!" And they pointed to the empty looms, for they believed that the others could see the cloth quite well.

"What!" said the emperor to himself. "I can see nothing! This is indeed horrible! Am I stupid? Am I not fit to be emperor?"

"Oh, very beautiful," he said. "It has my gracious approval." And he nodded pleasantly and examined the empty looms, for he would not say he could see nothing.

His whole court round him looked and looked and saw no more than the others;

but they said like the emperor, "Oh, it is beautiful!" And they advised him to wear the new and magnificent clothes to be made of it for the first time at the great procession which was soon to take place. "Splendid! Lovely! Most beautiful!" went from mouth to mouth. Everyone seemed delighted and the emperor gave to the impostors the title of Court Weavers to the Emperor.

Throughout the whole of the night before the morning on which the procession was to take place, the impostors were up and were working by the light of more than sixteen candles. The people could see that they were very busy making the emperor's new clothes ready. They pretended they were taking the cloth from the loom, were cutting with huge scissors in the air and were sewing with needles without thread, and then they said at last, "Now the clothes are finished!"

The emperor came himself with his most distinguished knights, and each impostor held up his arm just as if he were holding something, and said, "See, here are the breeches! Here is the coat! Here the cloak!" and so on.

"These clothes are so comfortable that one would imagine one had nothing on at all; but that is the beauty of it!"

"Yes," said all the knights, but they could see nothing, for there was nothing there.

"Will it please Your Majesty graciously to take off your clothes," said the impostors, "Then we will dress you in the new clothes, here before the mirror."

The emperor took off all his clothes, and the impostors placed themselves before him as if they were putting on each part of his new clothes which was ready, and the emperor turned and bent himself in front of the mirror.

"How beautifully they fit! How well they sit!" said everybody. "What material! What colors! Such a gorgeous suit!"

"They are waiting outside with the canopy which Your Majesty is wont to have borne over you in the processions," announced the Master of Ceremonies.

"Look, I am ready," said the emperor. "Doesn't it sit well!" And he turned himself again in the mirror to see if his finery was on all right.

The chamberlains put their hands near the floor as if they were lifting up the train. Then they acted as if they were holding something in the air. They would not have it noticed that they could see nothing.

So the emperor went along in the procession under the splendid canopy, and all the people in the streets and at the windows said, "How matchless are the emperor's new clothes! The train fastened to his dress, how beautifully it hangs!"

No one wished it to be noticed that he could see nothing, for then he would have been unfit for his office or else very stupid. None of the emperor's clothes had met with such approval as had these.

"But he has nothing on!" said a little child at last.

"Just listen to the innocent child!" said the father, and each one whispered to his neighbor what the child had said.

"But he has nothing on!" the whole of the people called out at last.

The emperor heard and it seemed to him they were right but he thought, I must go on with the procession now. And the chamberlains walked along still more uprightly, holding up the train which was not there at all.

Old MacDonald Had a Farm

Old MacDonald had a farm, E I E I O.
And on this farm he had some chicks, E I E I O.
With a chick-chick here and a chick-chick there,
Here a chick, there a chick, everywhere a chick-chick.
Old MacDonald had a farm, E I E I O.

Old MacDonald had a farm, E I E I O.
And on this farm he had some ducks, E I E I O.
With a quack-quack here and a quack-quack there,
Here a quack, there a quack, everywhere a quack-quack.
Old MacDonald had a farm, E I E I O.

Old MacDonald had a farm, E I E I O.
And on this farm he had some pigs, E I E I O.
With a grunt-grunt here and a grunt-grunt there,
Here a grunt, there a grunt, everywhere a grunt-grunt.
Old Macdonald had a farm, E I E I O.

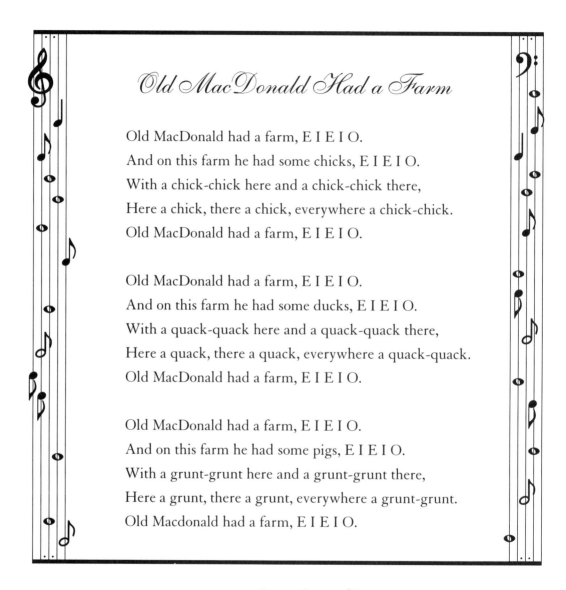

Pat a Cake, Pat a Cake, Baker's Man

Pat a cake, pat a cake, baker's man,
Please make me a cake, as fast as you can.
Pat it and prick it and mark it with B,
And put it in th'oven for Baby and me.

Snow-White and Rose-Red

BY THE BROTHERS GRIMM

THERE WAS ONCE a poor widow who lived in a lonely cottage. In front of the cottage was a garden wherein stood two rose-trees, one of which bore white and the other red roses. She had two children who were like the two rose-trees, and one was called Snow-white, and the other Rose-red. They were as good and happy, as busy and cheerful as ever two children in the world were, only Snow-white was more quiet and gentle than Rose-red. Rose-red liked better to run about in the meadows and fields seeking flowers and catching butterflies; but Snow-white sat at home with her mother, and helped her with her housework, or read to her when there was nothing to do.

The two children were so fond of one another that they always held each other by the hand when they went out together, and when Snow-white said: "We will not leave each other," Rose-red answered: "Never so long as we live," and their mother

would add: "What one has she must share with the other."

They often ran about the forest alone and gathered red berries, and no beasts did them any harm, but came close to them trustfully. The little hare would eat a cabbage-leaf out of their hands, the roe grazed by their side, the stag leapt merrily by them, and the birds sat still upon the boughs, and sang whatever they knew.

No mishap overtook them; if they had stayed too late in the forest, and night came on, they laid themselves down near one another upon the moss, and slept until morning came, and their mother knew this and did not worry on their account.

Once when they had spent the night in the wood and the dawn had roused them, they saw a beautiful child in a shining white dress sitting near their bed. He got up and looked quite kindly at them, but said nothing and went into the forest. And when they looked round they found that they had been sleeping quite close to a precipice, and would certainly have fallen into it in the darkness if they had gone only a few paces further. And their mother told them that it must have been the angel who watches over good children.

Snow-white and Rose-red kept their mother's little cottage so neat that it was a pleasure to look inside it. In the summer Rose-red took care of the house, and every morning laid a wreath of flowers by her mother's bed before she awoke, in which was a rose from each tree. In the winter Snow-white lit the fire and hung the kettle on the hob. The kettle was of brass and shone like gold, so brightly was it polished. In the evening, when the snowflakes fell, the mother said: "Go, Snow-white, and bolt the door," and then they sat round the hearth, and the mother took her spectacles and read aloud out of a large book, and the two girls listened as they sat and spun. And close by them lay a lamb upon the floor, and behind them upon a perch sat a white dove with its head hidden beneath its wings.

One evening, as they were thus sitting comfortably together, someone knocked at the door as if he wished to be let in. The mother said: "Quick, Rose-red, open the door, it must be a traveler who is seeking shelter." Rose-red went and pushed back the bolt, thinking that it was a poor man, but it was not; it was a bear that stretched his broad, black head within the door.

Rose-red screamed and sprang back, the lamb bleated, the dove fluttered, and Snow-white hid herself behind her mother's bed. But the bear began to speak and said: "Do not be afraid, I will do you no harm! I am half-frozen, and only want to warm myself a little beside you."

"Poor bear," said the mother, "lie down by the fire, only take care that you do not burn your coat." Then she cried: "Snow-white, Rose-red, come out, the bear will do you no harm, he means well." So they both came out, and by-and-by the lamb and dove came nearer, and were not afraid of him. The bear said: "Here, children, knock the snow out of my coat a little;" so they brought the broom and swept the bear's hide clean; and he stretched himself by the fire and growled contentedly and comfortably. It was not long before they grew quite at home, and played tricks with their clumsy guest. They tugged his hair with their hands, put their feet upon his back and rolled him about, or they took a hazel-switch and beat him, and when he growled they laughed. But the bear took it all in good part, only when they were too rough he called out:

> "Leave me alive, children,
> Snow-white, Rose-red,
> Will you beat your wooer dead?"

When it was bed-time and the others went to bed, the mother said to the bear: "You can lie there by the hearth, and then you will be safe from the cold and the bad weather." As soon as day dawned the two children let him out, and he trotted across the snow into the forest.

Henceforth the bear came every evening at the same time, laid himself down by the hearth, and let the children amuse themselves with him as much as they liked; and they got so used to him that the doors were never fastened until their black friend had arrived.

When spring had come and all outside was green, the bear said one morning to Snow-white: "Now I must go away, and cannot come back for the whole summer." "Where are you going, then, dear bear?" asked Snow-white. "I must go into the forest and guard my treasures from the wicked dwarfs. In the winter, when the earth is frozen hard, they are obliged to stay below and cannot work their way through; but now, when the sun has thawed and warmed the earth, they break through it, and come out to pry and steal; and what once gets into their hands, and in their caves, does not easily see daylight again."

Snow-white was quite sorry at his departure, and as she unbolted the door for him, and the bear was hurrying out, he caught against the bolt and a piece of his hairy coat was torn off, and it seemed to Snow-white as if she had seen gold shining through it, but she was not sure about it. The bear ran away quickly, and was soon out of sight behind the trees.

A short time afterwards the mother sent her children into the forest to get fire-wood. There they found a big tree which lay felled on the ground, and close by the trunk something was jumping backwards and forwards in the grass, but they could not make out what it was. When they came nearer they saw a dwarf with an old with-ered face and a snow-white beard a yard long. The end of the beard was caught in a crevice of the tree, and the little fellow was jumping about like a dog tied to a rope, and did not know what to do.

He glared at the girls with his fiery red eyes and cried: "Why do you stand there? Can you not come here and help me?" "What are you up to, little man?" asked Rose-red. "You stupid, prying goose!" answered the dwarf: "I was going to split the tree to get a little wood for cooking. The little bit of food that we people get is immediately burnt up with heavy logs; we do not swallow so much as you coarse, greedy folk. I had just driven the wedge safely in, and everything was going as I wished; but the cursed wedge was too smooth and suddenly sprang out, and the tree closed so quick-ly that I could not pull out my beautiful white beard; so now it is tight and I cannot get away, and the silly, sleek, milk-faced things laugh! Ugh! how odious you are!"

The children tried very hard, but they could not pull the beard out, it was caught too fast. "I will run and fetch someone," said Rose-red. "You senseless goose!" snarled

the dwarf; "Why should you fetch someone? You are already two too many for me; can you not think of something better?" "Don't be impatient," said Snow-white, "I will help you," and she pulled her scissors out of her pocket, and cut off the end of the beard.

As soon as the dwarf felt himself free he laid hold of a bag which lay amongst the roots of the tree, and which was full of gold, and lifted it up, grumbling to himself: "Uncouth people, to cut off a piece of my fine beard. Bad luck to you!" and then he swung the bag upon his back, and went off without even once looking at the children.

Some time afterwards Snow-white and Rose-red went to catch a dish of fish. As they came near the brook they saw something like a large grasshopper jumping towards the water, as if it were going to leap in. They ran to it and found it was the dwarf. "Where are you going?" said Rose-red; "you surely don't want to go into the water?" "I am not such a fool!" cried the dwarf; "don't you see that the accursed fish wants to pull me in?" The little man had been sitting there fishing, and unluckily the wind had tangled up his beard with the fishing-line; a moment later a big fish made a bite and the feeble creature had not strength to pull it out; the fish kept the upper hand and pulled the dwarf towards him. He held on to all the reeds and rushes, but it was of little good, for he was forced to follow the movements of the fish, and was in urgent danger of being dragged into the water.

The girls came just in time; they held him fast and tried to free his beard from the line, but all in vain, beard and line were entangled fast together. There was nothing to do but to bring out the scissors and cut the beard, whereby a small part of it was lost. When the dwarf saw that he screamed out: "Is that civil, you toadstool, to disfigure a man's face? Was it not enough to clip off the end of my beard? Now you have cut off the best part of it. I cannot let myself be seen by my people. I wish you had been made to run the soles off your shoes!" Then he took out a sack of pearls which lay in the rushes, and without another word he dragged it away and disappeared behind a stone.

It happened that soon afterwards the mother sent the two children to the town to buy needles and thread, and laces and ribbons. The road led them across a heath upon which huge pieces of rock lay strewn about. There they noticed a large bird hovering in the air, flying slowly round and round above them; it sank lower and lower, and at last settled near a rock not far away. Immediately they heard a loud, piteous cry. They ran up and saw with horror that the eagle had seized their old acquaintance the dwarf, and was going to carry him off.

The children, full of pity, at once took tight hold of the little man, and pulled against the eagle so long that at last he let his booty go. As soon as the dwarf had recovered from his first fright he cried with his shrill voice: "Could you not have done it more carefully! You dragged at my brown coat so that it is all torn and full of holes, you clumsy creatures!" Then he took up a sack full of precious stones, and slipped away again under the rock into his hole. The girls, who by this time were used to his ingratitude, went on their way and did their business in the town.

As they crossed the heath again on their way home they surprised the dwarf, who had emptied out his bag of precious stones in a clean spot, and had not thought that anyone would come there so late. The evening sun shone upon the brilliant stones; they glittered and sparkled with all colours so beautifully that the children stood still and stared at them. "Why do you stand gaping there?" cried the dwarf, and his ashen-grey face became copper-red with rage. He was still cursing when a loud growling was heard, and a black bear came trotting towards them out of the forest. The dwarf sprang up in a fright, but he could not reach his cave, for the bear was already close. Then in the dread of his heart he cried: "Dear Mr. Bear, spare me, I will give you all my treasures; look, the beautiful jewels lying there! Grant me my life; what do you want with such a slender little fellow as I? You would not feel me between your teeth. Come, take these two wicked girls, they are tender morsels for you, fat as young quails; for mercy's sake eat them!" The bear took no heed of his words, but gave the wicked creature a single blow with his paw, and he did not move again.

The girls had run away, but the bear called to them: "Snow-white and Rose-red, do not be afraid; wait, I will come with you." Then they recognized his voice and waited, and when he came up to them suddenly his bearskin fell off, and he stood there a handsome man, clothed all in gold. "I am a king's son," he said, "And I was bewitched by that wicked dwarf, who had stolen my treasures; I have had to run about the forest as a savage bear until I was freed by his death. Now he has got his well-deserved punishment.

Snow-white was married to him, and Rose-red to his brother, and they divided between them the great treasure which the dwarf had gathered together in his cave. The old mother lived peacefully and happily with her children for many years. She took the two rose-trees with her, and they stood before her window, and every year bore the most beautiful roses, white and red.

Sing a Song of Sixpence

Sing a song of sixpence,
    a pocket full of rye.
Four and twenty blackbirds
    baked in a pie;
When the pie was open'd
    the birds began to sing,
Wasn't that a dainty dish to set before a king?

The King was in his counting house,
    counting out his money,
The queen was in the parlor,
    eating bread and honey.

The maid was in the garden,
    hanging out the clothes,
There came a little blackbird,
    and snapped at her nose.

Jack and the Beanstalk

BY JOSEPH JACOBS

JACK SELLS THE COW

ONCE UPON A TIME there was a poor widow who lived in a little cottage with her only son Jack.

Jack was a giddy, thoughtless boy, but very kind-hearted and affectionate. There had been a hard winter, and after it the poor woman had suffered from fever and ague. Jack did not work as yet, and by degrees they grew dreadfully poor. The widow saw that there was no means of keeping Jack and herself from starvation but by selling her cow; so one morning she said to her son, "I am too weak to go myself, Jack, so you must take the cow to market for me, and sell her."

Jack liked going to market to sell the cow very much; but as he was on the way, he met a butcher who had some beautiful beans in his hand. Jack stopped to look at them, and the butcher told the boy that they were of great value, and persuaded the silly lad to sell the cow for these beans.

When he brought them home to his mother instead of the money she expected for her nice cow, she was very vexed and shed many tears, scolding Jack for his folly. He was very sorry, and mother and son went to bed very sadly that night; their last hope seemed gone.

At daybreak Jack rose and went into the garden.

"At least," he thought, "I will sow the wonderful beans. Mother says that they are just common scarlet-runners, and nothing else; but I may as well sow them."

So he took a piece of stick, and made some holes in the ground, and put in the beans.

That day they had very little dinner, and went sadly to bed, knowing that for the next day there would be none and Jack, unable to sleep from grief and vexation, got up at day-dawn and went out into the garden.

What was his amazement to find that the beans had grown up in the night, and climbed up and up till they covered the high cliff that sheltered the cottage, and disappeared above it! The stalks had twined and twisted themselves till they formed quite a ladder.

"It would be easy to climb it," thought Jack.

And, having thought of the experiment, he at once resolved to carry it out, for Jack was a good climber. However, after his late mistake about the cow, he thought he had better consult his mother first.

WONDERFUL GROWTH OF THE BEANSTALK

So Jack called his mother, and they both gazed in silent wonder at the Beanstalk, which was not only of great height, but was thick enough to bear Jack's weight.

"I wonder where it ends," said Jack to his mother; "I think I will climb up and see."

His mother wished him not to venture up this strange ladder, but Jack coaxed her to give her consent to the attempt, for he was certain there must be something wonderful in the Beanstalk; so at last she yielded to his wishes.

Jack instantly began to climb, and went up and up on the ladderlike bean till everything he had left behind him—the cottage, the village, and even the tall church tower—looked quite little, and still he could not see the top of the Beanstalk.

Jack felt a little tired, and thought for a moment that he would go back again; but he was a very persevering boy, and he knew that the way to succeed in anything is not to give up. So after resting for a moment he went on.

After climbing higher and higher, till he grew afraid to look down for fear he should be giddy, Jack at last reached the top of the Beanstalk, and found himself in a beautiful country, finely wooded, with beautiful meadows covered with sheep. A crystal stream ran through the pastures; not far from the place where he had got off the Beanstalk stood a fine, strong castle.

Jack wondered very much that he had never heard of or seen this castle before; but when he reflected on the subject, he saw that it was as much separated from the village by the perpendicular rock on which it stood as if it were in another land.

While Jack was standing looking at the castle, a very strange-looking woman came out of the wood, and advanced towards him.

She wore a pointed cap of quilted red satin turned up with ermine, her hair streamed loose over her shoulders, and she walked with a staff. Jack took off his cap and made her a bow.

"If you please, ma'am," said he, "is this your house?"

"No," said the old lady. "Listen, and I will tell you the story of that castle.

"Once upon a time there was a noble knight, who lived in this castle, which is on the borders of Fairyland. He had a fair and beloved wife and several lovely children: and as his neighbours, the little people, were very friendly towards him, they bestowed on him many excellent and precious gifts.

"Rumour whispered of these treasures; and a monstrous giant, who lived at no great distance, and who was a very wicked being, resolved to obtain possession of them.

"So he bribed a false servant to let him inside the castle, when the knight was in bed and asleep, and he killed him as he lay. Then he went to the part of the castle which was the nursery, and also killed all the poor little ones he found there.

"Happily for her, the lady was not to be found. She had gone with her infant son, who was only two or three months old, to visit her old nurse, who lived in the valley; and she had been detained all night there by a storm.

"The next morning, as soon as it was light, one of the servants at the castle, who had managed to escape, came to tell the poor lady of the sad fate of her husband and her pretty babes. She could scarcely believe him at first, and was eager at once to go back and share the fate of her dear ones; but the old nurse, with many tears, besought her to remember that she had still a child, and that it was her duty to preserve her life for the sake of the poor innocent.

"The lady yielded to this reasoning, and consented to remain at her nurse's house as the best place of concealment; for the servant told her that the giant had vowed, if he could find her, he would kill both her and her baby. Years rolled on. The old nurse died, leaving her cottage and the few articles of furniture it contained to her poor lady, who dwelt in it, working as a peasant for her daily bread. Her spinning-wheel and the milk of a cow, which she had purchased with the little money she had with her, sufficed for the scanty subsistence of herself and her little son. There was a nice little garden attached to the cottage, in which they cultivated peas, beans, and cabbages, and the lady was not ashamed to go out at harvest time, and glean in the fields to supply her little son's wants.

"Jack, that poor lady is your mother. This castle was once your father's, and must again be yours."

Jack uttered a cry of surprise.

"My mother! oh, madam, what ought I to do? My poor father! My dear mother!"

"Your duty requires you to win it back for your mother. But the task is a very difficult one, and full of peril, Jack. Have you courage to undertake it?"

"I fear nothing when I am doing right," said Jack.

"Then," said the lady in the red cap, "You are one of those who slay giants. You must get into the castle, and if possible possess yourself of a hen that lays golden eggs, and a harp that talks. Remember, all the giant possesses is really yours." As she ceased speaking, the lady of the red hat suddenly disappeared, and of course Jack knew she was a fairy.

Jack determined at once to attempt the adventure; so he advanced, and blew the horn which hung at the castle portal. The door was opened in a minute or two by a frightful giantess, with one great eye in the middle of her forehead.

As soon as Jack saw her he turned to run away, but she caught him, and dragged him into the castle.

"Ho, ho!" she laughed terribly. "You didn't expect to see me here, that is clear! No, I shan't let you go again. I am weary of my life. I am so overworked, and I don't see why I should not have a page as well as other ladies. And you shall be my boy. You shall clean the knives, and black the boots, and make the fires, and help me generally when the giant is out. When he is at home I must hide you, for he has eaten up all my pages hitherto, and you would be a dainty morsel, my little lad."

While she spoke she dragged Jack right into the castle. The poor boy was very much frightened, as I am sure you and I would have been in his place. But he remembered that fear disgraces a man; so he struggled to be brave and make the best of things.

"I am quite ready to help you, and do all I can to serve you, madam," he said, "only I beg you will be good enough to hide me from your husband, for I should not like to be eaten at all."

"That's a good boy," said the Giantess, nodding her head; "it is lucky for you that you did not scream out when you saw me, as the other boys who have been here did, for if you had done so my husband would have awakened and have eaten you, as he did them, for breakfast. Come here, child; go into my wardrobe: he never ventures to open that; you will be safe there."

And she opened a huge wardrobe which stood in the great hall, and shut him into it. But the keyhole was so large that it admitted plenty of air, and he could see everything that took place through it. By-and-by he heard a heavy tramp on the stairs, like the lumbering along of a great cannon, and then a voice like thunder cried out:

> "Fe, fa, fi-fo-fum,
> I smell the breath of an Englishman.
> Let him be alive or let him be dead,
> I'll grind his bones to make my bread."

"Wife," cried the Giant, "there is a man in the castle. Let me have him for breakfast."

"You are grown old and stupid," cried the lady in her loud tones. "It is only a nice fresh steak off an elephant, that I have cooked for you, which you smell. There, sit down and make a good breakfast."

And she placed a huge dish before him of savoury steaming meat, which greatly pleased him, and made him forget his idea of an Englishman being in the castle. When he had breakfasted he went out for a walk; and then the Giantess opened the door, and made Jack come out to help her. He helped her all day. She fed him well, and when evening came put him back in the wardrobe.

The Giant came in to supper. Jack watched him through the keyhole, and was amazed to see him pick a wolf's bones and put half a fowl at a time into his capacious mouth.

When the supper was ended he bade his wife bring him his hen that laid the golden eggs.

"It lays as well as it did when it belonged to that paltry knight," he said; "indeed I think the eggs are heavier than ever."

The Giantess went away, and soon returned with a little brown hen, which she placed on the table before her husband. "And now, my dear," she said, "I am going for a walk, if you don't want me any longer."

"Go," said the Giant; "I shall be glad to have a nap by-and-by."

Then he took up the brown hen and said to her:

"Lay!" And she instantly laid a golden egg.

"Lay!" said the Giant again. And she laid another.

"Lay!" he repeated the third time. And again a golden egg lay on the table.

Now Jack was sure this hen was that of which the fairy had spoken.

By-and-by the Giant put the hen down on the floor, and soon after went fast asleep, snoring so loud that it sounded like thunder.

Directly Jack perceived that the Giant was fast asleep, he pushed open the door of the wardrobe and crept out; very softly he stole across the room, and picking up the hen, made haste to quit the apartment. He knew the way to the kitchen, the door of which he found was left ajar; he opened it, shut and locked it after him, and flew back to the Beanstalk, which he descended as fast as his feet would move.

When his mother saw him enter the house she wept for joy, for she had feared that the fairies had carried him away, or that the Giant had found him. But Jack put the brown hen down before her, and told her how he had been in the Giant's castle, and all his adventures. She was very glad to see the hen, which would make them rich once more.

THE MONEY BAGS

Jack made another journey up the Beanstalk to the Giant's castle one day while his mother had gone to market; but first he dyed his hair and disguised himself. The old woman did not know him again, and dragged him in as she had done before, to help her to do the work; but she heard her husband coming, and hid him in the wardrobe, not thinking that it was the same boy who had stolen the hen. She bade him stay quite still there, or the Giant would eat him.

Then the Giant came in saying:

> "Fe, fa, fi-fo-fum,
> I smell the breath of an Englishman.
> Let him be alive or let him be dead,
> I'll grind his bones to make my bread."

"Nonsense!" said the wife, "it is only a roasted bullock that I thought would be a tit-bit for your supper; sit down and I will bring it up at once." The Giant sat down, and soon his wife brought up a roasted bullock on a large dish, and they began their supper. Jack was amazed to see them pick the bones of the bullock as if it had been a lark. As soon as they had finished their meal, the Giantess rose and said:

"Now, my dear, with your leave I am going up to my room to finish the story I am reading. If you want me call for me."

"First," answered the Giant, "bring me my money bags, that I may count my golden pieces before I sleep." The Giantess obeyed. She went and soon returned with two large bags over her shoulders, which she put down by her husband.

"There," she said; "that is all that is left of the knight's money. When you have spent it you must go and take another baron's castle."

"That he shan't, if I can help it," thought jack.

The Giant, when his wife was gone, took out heaps and heaps of golden pieces, and counted them, and put them in piles, till he was tired of the amusement. Then he swept them all back into their bags, and leaning back in his chair fell fast asleep, snoring so loud that no other sound was audible.

Jack stole softly out of the wardrobe, and taking up the bags of money (which were his very own, because the Giant had stolen them from his father), he ran off, and with great difficulty descending the Beanstalk, laid the bags of gold on his mother's table. She had just returned from town, and was crying at not finding Jack.

"There, mother, I have brought you the gold that my father lost."

"Oh, Jack! you are a very good boy, but I wish you would not risk your precious life in the Giant's castle. Tell me how you came to go there again."

And Jack told her all about it.

Jack's mother was very glad to get the money, but she did not like him to run any risk for her.

But after a time Jack made up his mind to go again to the Giant's castle.

THE TALKING HARP

So he climbed the Beanstalk once more, and blew the horn at the Giant's gate. The Giantess soon opened the door; she was very stupid, and did not know him again, but she stopped a minute before she took him in. She feared another robbery; but Jack's fresh face looked so innocent that she could not resist him, and so she bade him come in, and again hid him away in the wardrobe.

By-and-by the Giant came home, and as soon as he had crossed the threshold he roared out:

> "Fe, fa, fi-fo-fum,
> I smell the breath of an Englishman.
> Let him be alive or let him be dead,
> I'll grind his bones to make my bread."

"You stupid old Giant," said his wife, "you only smell a nice sheep, which I have grilled for your dinner."

And the Giant sat down, and his wife brought up a whole sheep for his dinner. When he had eaten it all up, he said:

"Now bring me my harp, and I will have a little music while you take your walk."

The Giantess obeyed, and returned with a beautiful harp. The framework was all sparkling with diamonds and rubies, and the strings were all of gold.

"This is one of the nicest things I took from the knight," said the Giant. "I am very fond of music, and my harp is a faithful servant."

So he drew the harp towards him, and said:

"Play!"

And the harp played a very soft, sad air.

"Play something merrier!" said the Giant.

And the harp played a merry tune.

"Now play me a lullaby," roared the Giant; and the harp played a sweet lullaby, to the sound of which its master fell asleep.

Then Jack stole softly out of the wardrobe, and went into the huge kitchen to see if the Giantess had gone out; he found no one there, so he went to the door and opened it softly, for he thought he could not do so with the harp in his hand.

Then he entered the Giant's room and seized the harp and ran away with it; but as he jumped over the threshold the harp called out:

"Master! Master!"

And the Giant woke up.

With a tremendous roar he sprang from his seat, and in two strides had reached the door.

But Jack was very nimble. He fled like lightning with the harp, talking to it as he went (for he saw it was a fairy), and telling it he was the son of its old master, the knight.

Still the Giant came on so fast that he was quite close to poor Jack, and had stretched out his great hand to catch him. But, luckily, just at that moment he stepped upon a loose stone, stumbled, and fell flat on the ground, where he lay at his full length.

This accident gave Jack time to get on the Beanstalk and hasten down it; but just as he reached their own garden he beheld the Giant descending after him.

"Mother! mother!" cried Jack, "make haste and give me the axe."

His mother ran to him with a hatchet in her hand, and Jack with one tremendous blow cut through all the Beanstalks except one.

"Now, mother, stand out of the way!" said he.

THE GIANT BREAKS HIS NECK

Jack's mother shrank back, and it was well she did so, for just as the Giant took hold of the last branch of the Beanstalk, Jack cut the stem quite through and darted from the spot.

Down came the Giant with a terrible crash, and as he fell on his head, he broke his neck, and lay dead at the feet of the woman he had so much injured.

Before Jack and his mother had recovered from their alarm and agitation, a beautiful lady stood before them.

"Jack," said she, "you have acted like a brave knight's son, and deserve to have your inheritance restored to you. Dig a grave and bury the Giant, and then go and kill the Giantess."

"But," said Jack, "I could not kill anyone unless I were fighting with him; and I could not draw my sword upon a woman. Moreover, the Giantess was very kind to me."

The Fairy smiled on Jack.

"I am very much pleased with your generous feeling," she said. "Nevertheless, return to the castle, and act as you will find needful."

Jack asked the Fairy if she would show him the way to the castle, as the Beanstalk was now down. She told him that she would drive him there in her chariot, which was drawn by two peacocks. Jack thanked her, and sat down in the chariot with her.

The Fairy drove him a long distance round, till they reached a village which lay at the bottom of the hill. Here they found a number of miserable-looking men assembled. The Fairy stopped her carriage and addressed them:

"My friends," said she, "the cruel giant who oppressed you and ate up all your flocks and herds is dead, and this young gentleman was the means of your being delivered from him, and is the son of your kind old master, the knight."

The men gave a loud cheer at these words, and pressed forward to say that they would serve Jack as faithfully as they had served his father. The Fairy bade them follow her to the castle, and they marched thither in a body, and Jack blew the horn and demanded admittance.

The old Giantess saw them coming from the turret loop-hole. She was very much frightened, for she guessed that something had happened to her husband; and as she came downstairs very fast she caught her foot in her dress, and fell from the top to the bottom and broke her neck.

When the people outside found that the door was not opened to them, they took crowbars and forced the portal. Nobody was to be seen, but on leaving the hall they found the body of the Giantess at the foot of the stairs.

Thus Jack took possession of the castle. The Fairy went and brought his mother to him, with the hen and the harp. He had the Giantess buried, and endeavoured as much as lay in his power to do right to those whom the Giant had robbed.

Before her departure for fairyland, the Fairy explained to Jack that she had sent the butcher to meet him with the beans, in order to try what sort of lad he was.

"If you had looked at the gigantic Beanstalk and only stupidly wondered about it," she said, "I should have left you where misfortune had placed you, only restoring her cow to your mother. But you showed an inquiring mind, and great courage and enterprise, therefore you deserve to rise; and when you mounted the Beanstalk you climbed the Ladder of Fortune."

She then took her leave of Jack and his mother.

Pop! Goes the Weasel

All around the cobbler's bench,
The monkey chased the weasel;
The monkey thought 'twas all in fun,
    Pop! goes the weasel.

I've no time to wait or sigh,
No patience to wait till bye and bye;
Kiss me quick, I'm off; good-bye,
    Pop! goes the weasel.

A penny for a spool of thread,
A penny for a needle,
That's the way the money goes,
    Pop! goes the weasel.

Johnny's got the whooping cough
And Jenny's got the measles,
That's the way the money goes,
Pop! goes the weasel.

The butcher, when he charges for meat,
Sticks in the bone and gristle,
But that's the way the money goes,
Pop! goes the weasel.

The painter works with ladder and brush,
The artist with the easel,
The fiddler always snaps the strings,
Pop! goes the weasel.

I've Been Working On The Railroad

I've been working on the railroad,
All the live-long day,
I've been working on the railroad,
Just to pass the time away.
Don't you hear the whistle blowing,
Rise up so early in the morn;
Don't you hear the captain shouting,
"Dinah, blow your horn!"

Dinah, won't you blow, Dinah, won't you blow,
Dinah, won't you blow your horn.
Dinah, won't you blow, Dinah, won't you blow,
Dinah, won't you blow your horn.

Someone's in the kitchen with Dinah,
Someone's in the kitchen I know,
Someone's in the kitchen with Dinah,
Strum-min' on the old banjo, and singin':

Fee - fi - fidd - lee - i - o,
Fee - fi - fidd - lee- i o,
Fee - fi - fidd - lee - i - o,
Strummin' on the old banjo.

Rumpelstiltskin

BY THE BROTHERS GRIMM

BY THE SIDE OF A WOOD, in a country a long way off, ran a fine stream of water; and upon the stream there stood a mill. The miller's house was close by, and the miller, you must know, had a very beautiful daughter. She was, moreover, very shrewd and clever; and the miller was so proud of her, that he one day told the king of the land, who used to come and hunt in the wood, that his daughter could spin gold out of straw. Now this king was very fond of money; and when he heard the miller's boast his greediness was raised, and he sent for the girl to be brought before him. Then he led her to a chamber in his palace where there was a great heap of straw, and gave her a spinning-wheel, and said, "All this must be spun into gold before morning, as you love your life." It was in vain that the poor maiden said that it was only a silly boast of her father, for that she could do no such thing as spin straw into gold: the chamber door was locked, and she was left alone.

She sat down in one corner of the room, and began to bewail her hard fate; when on a sudden the door opened, and a droll-looking little man hobbled in, and said, "Good morrow to you, my good lass; what are you weeping for?" "Alas!" said she, "I must spin this straw into gold, and I know not how." "What will you give me," said the hobgoblin, "to do it for you?" "My necklace," replied the maiden. He took her at her word, and sat himself down to the wheel, and whistled and sang:

> *"Round about, round about,*
> *Lo, and behold!*
> *Reel away, reel away,*
> *Straw into gold!"*

And round about the wheel went merrily; the work was quickly done, and the straw was all spun into gold.

When the king came and saw this, he was greatly astonished and pleased; but his heart grew still more greedy of gain, and he shut up the poor miller's daughter again with a fresh task. Then she knew not what to do, and sat down once more to weep; but the dwarf soon opened the door, and said, "What will you give me to do your task?" "The ring on my finger," said she. So her little friend took the ring, and began to work at the wheel again, and whistled and sang:

> *"Round about, round about,*
> *Lo and behold!*
> *Reel away, reel away,*
> *Straw into gold!"*

till, long before morning, all was done again.

The king was greatly delighted to see all this glittering treasure; but still he had not enough: so he took the miller's daughter to a yet larger heap, and said, "All this must be spun tonight; and if it is, you shall be my queen." As soon as she was alone the dwarf came in, and said, "What will you give me to spin gold for you this third time?" "I have nothing left," said she. "Then say you will give me," said the little man, "the first little child that you may have when you are queen." "That may never be," thought the miller's daughter: and as she knew no other way to get her task done, she said she would do what he asked. Round went the wheel again to the old song, and the manikin once more spun the heap into gold. The king came in the morning, and, finding all he wanted, was forced to keep his word; so he married the miller's daughter, and she really became queen.

At the birth of her first little child she was very glad, and forgot the dwarf, and what she had said. But one day he came into her room, where she was sitting playing with her baby, and put her in mind of it. Then she grieved sorely at her misfortune, and said she would give him all the wealth of the kingdom if he would let her off, but in vain; till at last her tears softened him, and he said, "I will give you three days' grace, and if during that time you tell me my name, you shall keep your child."

Now the queen lay awake all night, thinking of all the odd names that she had ever heard; and she sent messengers all over the land to find out new ones. The next day the little man came, and she began with Timothy, Ichabod, Benjamin, Jeremiah, and all the names she could remember; but to all and each of them he said, "Madam, that is not my name."

The second day she began with all the comical names she could hear of, Bandy-legs, Hunchback, Crook-shanks, and so on; but the little gentleman still said to every one of them, "Madam, that is not my name."

The third day one of the messengers came back, and said, "I have traveled two days without hearing of any other names; but yesterday, as I was climbing a high hill, among the trees of the forest where the fox and the hare bid each other good night, I saw a little hut; and before the hut burnt a fire; and round about the fire a funny little dwarf was dancing upon one leg, and singing:

> " 'Merrily the feast I'll make.
> Today I'll brew, tomorrow bake;
> Merrily I'll dance and sing,
> For next day will a stranger bring.
> Little does my lady dream
> Rumpelstiltskin is my name!' "

When the queen heard this she jumped for joy, and as soon as her little friend came she sat down upon her throne, and called all her court round to enjoy the fun; and the nurse stood by her side with the baby in her arms, as if it was quite ready to be given up. Then the little man began to chuckle at the thought of having the poor child, to take home with him to his hut in the woods; and he cried out, "Now, lady, what is my name?" "Is it John?" asked she. "No, madam!" "Is it Tom?" "No, madam!" "Is it Jemmy?" "It is not." "Can your name be Rumpelstiltskin?" said the lady slyly. "Some witch told you that!—some witch told you that!" cried the little man, and dashed his right foot in a rage so deep into the floor, that he was forced to lay hold of it with both hands to pull it out.

Then he made the best of his way off, while the nurse laughed and the baby crowed; and all the court jeered at him for having had so much trouble for nothing, and said, "We wish you a very good morning, and a merry feast, Mr. Rumpelstiltskin!"

Hickory Dickory Dock

Hickory, dickory, dock!
The mouse ran up the clock,
The clock struck one,
And down it ran,
Hickory, dickory, dock!

Hickory, dickory, dock,
The mouse ran up the clock,
The clock struck three
The mouse ran away,
Hickory, dickory, dock.

Hickory, dickory, dock,
The mouse ran up the clock,
The clock struck ten,
The mouse came again,
Hickory, dickory, dock.

Little Red Riding-Hood

BY CHARLES PERRAULT

ONCE UPON A TIME there lived in a certain village a little country girl, the prettiest creature was ever seen. Her mother was excessively fond of her; and her grandmother doted on her still more. This good woman got made for her a little red riding-hood; which became the girl so extremely well that everybody called her Little Red Riding-Hood.

One day her mother, having made some custards, said to her:

"Go, my dear, and see how thy grandmamma does, for I hear she has been very ill; carry her a custard, and this little pot of butter."

Little Red Riding-Hood set out immediately to go to her grandmother, who lived in another village.

As she was going through the wood, she met with Gaffer Wolf, who had a very great mind to eat her up, but he durst not, because of some faggot-makers hard by in the forest. He asked her whither she was going. The poor child, who did not know that it was dangerous to stay and hear a wolf talk, said to him:

"I am going to see my grandmamma and carry her a custard and a little pot of butter from my mamma."

"Does she live far off?" said the Wolf.

"Oh! ay," answered Little Red Riding-Hood; "it is beyond that mill you see there, at the first house in the village."

"Well," said the Wolf, "and I'll go and see her too. I'll go this way and go you that, and we shall see who will be there soonest."

The Wolf began to run as fast as he could, taking the nearest way, and the little girl went by that farthest about, diverting herself in gathering nuts, running after butterflies, and making nosegays of such little flowers as she met with. The Wolf was not long before he got to the old woman's house. He knocked at the door—tap, tap.

"Who's there?"

"Your grandchild, Little Red Riding-Hood," replied the Wolf, counterfeiting her voice; "who has brought you a custard and a little pot of butter sent you by mamma."

The good grandmother, who was in bed, because she was somewhat ill, cried out:

"Pull the bobbin, and the latch will go up."

The Wolf pulled the bobbin, and the door opened, and then presently he fell upon the good woman and ate her up in a moment, for it was above three days that he had not touched a bit. He then shut the door and went into the grandmother's bed, expecting Little Red Riding-Hood, who came some time afterwards and knocked at the door—tap, tap.

"Who's there?"

Little Red Riding-Hood, hearing the big voice of the Wolf, was at first afraid; but believing her grandmother had got a cold and was hoarse, answered:

" 'Tis your grandchild Little Red Riding-Hood, who has brought you a custard and a little pot of butter mamma sends you."

The Wolf cried out to her, softening his voice as much as he could:

"Pull the bobbin, and the latch will go up."

Little Red Riding-Hood pulled the bobbin, and the door opened.

The Wolf, seeing her come in, said to her, hiding himself under the bed-clothes:

"Put the custard and the little pot of butter upon the stool, and come and lie down with me."

Little Red Riding-Hood undressed herself and went into bed, where, being greatly amazed to see how her grandmother looked in her night-clothes, she said to her:

"Grandmamma, what great arms you have got!"

"That is the better to hug thee, my dear."

"Grandmamma, what great legs you have got!"

"That is to run the better, my child."

"Grandmamma, what great ears you have got!"

"That is to hear the better, my child."

"Grandmamma, what great eyes you have got!"

"It is to see the better, my child."

"Grandmamma, what great teeth you have got!"

"That is to eat thee up."

And, saying these words, this wicked wolf fell upon Little Red Riding-Hood, and ate her all up.

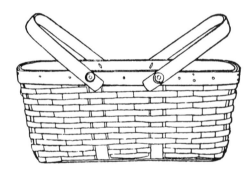

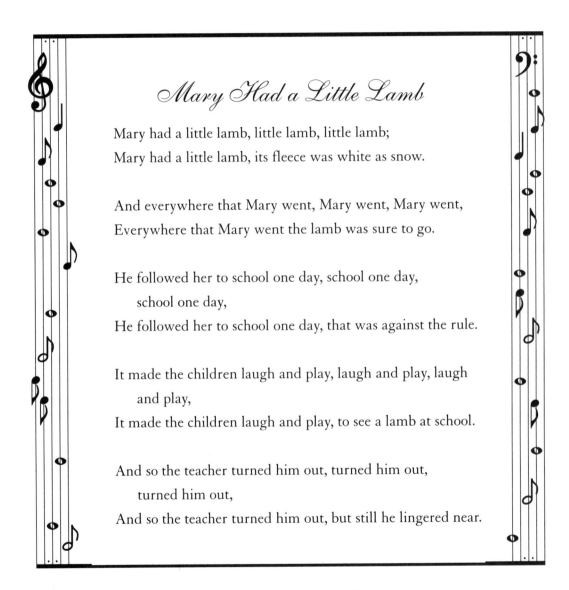

Mary Had a Little Lamb

Mary had a little lamb, little lamb, little lamb;
Mary had a little lamb, its fleece was white as snow.

And everywhere that Mary went, Mary went, Mary went,
Everywhere that Mary went the lamb was sure to go.

He followed her to school one day, school one day,
    school one day,
He followed her to school one day, that was against the rule.

It made the children laugh and play, laugh and play, laugh
    and play,
It made the children laugh and play, to see a lamb at school.

And so the teacher turned him out, turned him out,
    turned him out,
And so the teacher turned him out, but still he lingered near.

He waited patiently about, patiently, patiently,
He waited patiently about, till Mary did appear.

What makes the lamb love Mary so, Mary so, Mary so,
What makes the lamb love Mary so, the eager children cry.

Mary loves the lamb you know, lamb you know,
  lamb you know,
O, Mary loves the lamb you know, the teacher did reply.

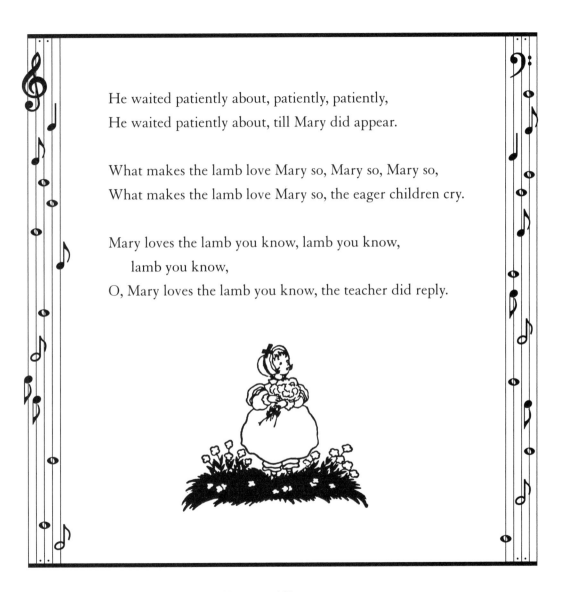

ONE FINE EVENING a young princess put on her bonnet and clogs, and went out to take a walk by herself in a wood; and when she came to a cool spring of water, that rose in the midst of it, she sat herself down to rest a while. Now she had a golden ball in her hand, which was her favourite plaything; and she was always tossing it up into the air, and catching it again as it fell. After a time she threw it up so high that she missed catching it as it fell; and the ball bounded away, and rolled along upon the ground, till at last it fell down into the spring. The princess looked into the spring after her ball, but it was very deep, so deep that she could not see the bottom of it. Then she began to bewail her loss, and said, "Alas! if I could only get my ball again, I would give all my fine clothes and jewels, and everything that I have in the world."

Whilst she was speaking, a frog put its head out of the water, and said,

"Princess, why do you weep so bitterly?" "Alas!" said she, "what can you do for me, you nasty frog? My golden ball has fallen into the spring." The frog said, "I want not your pearls, and jewels, and fine clothes; but if you will love me, and let me live with you and eat from off your golden plate, and sleep upon your bed, I will bring you your ball again." "What nonsense," thought the princess, "this silly frog is talking! He can never even get out of the spring to visit me, though he may be able to get my ball for me, and therefore I will tell him he shall have what he asks." So she said to the frog, "Well, if you bring me my ball, I will do all you ask." Then the frog put his head down, and dived deep under the water; and after a little while he came up again, with the ball in his mouth, and threw it on the edge of the spring. As soon as the young princess saw her ball, she ran to pick it up; and she was so overjoyed to have it in her hand again, that she never thought of the frog, but ran home with it as fast as she could. The frog called after her, "Stay, princess, and take me with you as you said," But she did not stop to hear a word.

The next day, just as the princess had sat down to dinner, she heard a strange noise — tap, tap — plash, plash — as if something was coming up the marble staircase: and soon afterwards there was a gentle knock at the door, and a little voice cried out and said:

> "Open the door, my princess dear,
> Open the door to thy true love here!
> And mind the words that thou and I said
> By the fountain cool, in the greenwood shade."

Then the princess ran to the door and opened it, and there she saw the frog, whom she had quite forgotten. At this sight she was sadly frightened, and shutting the door as fast as she could came back to her seat. The king, her father, seeing that something had frightened her, asked her what was the matter. "There is a nasty frog," said she, "at the door, that lifted my ball for me out of the spring this morning: I told him that he should live with me here, thinking that he could never get out of the spring; but there he is at the door, and he wants to come in."

While she was speaking the frog knocked again at the door, and said:

> "Open the door, my princess dear,
> Open the door to thy true love here!
> And mind the words that thou and I said
> By the fountain cool, in the greenwood shade."

Then the king said to the young princess, "As you have given your word you must keep it; so go and let him in." She did so, and the frog hopped into the room, and then straight on — tap, tap — plash, plash — from the bottom of the room to the top, till he came up close to a table where the princess sat. "Pray lift me upon a chair," said he to the princess, "and let me sit next to you." As soon as she had done this, the frog said, "Put your plate nearer to me, that I may eat out of it." This she did, and when he had eaten as much as he could, he said, "Now I am tired; carry me upstairs, and put me into your bed." And the princess, though very unwilling, took him up in her hand, and put him upon the pillow of her own bed, where he slept all night long.

As soon as it was light he humped up, hopped downstairs, and went out of the house. "Now, then," thought the princess, "at last he is gone, and I shall be troubled with him no more."

But she was mistaken; for when night came again she heard the same tapping at the door; and the frog came once more, and said:

> "Open the door, my princess dear,
> Open the door to thy true love here!
> And mind the words that thou and I said
> By the fountain cool, in the greenwood shade."

And when the princess opened the door the frog came in, and slept upon her pillow as before, till the morning broke. And the third night he did just the same. But when the princess awoke on the following morning she was astonished to see, instead of the frog, a handsome prince, gazing on her with the most beautiful eyes she had ever seen, and standing at the head of her bed.

He told her that he had been enchanted by a spiteful fairy, who had changed him into a frog; and that he had been fated so to abide till some princess should take him out of the spring, and let him eat from her plate, and sleep upon her bed for three nights. "You," said the prince, "have broken his cruel charm, and now I have nothing to wish for but that you should go with me into my father's kingdom, where I will marry you, and love you as long as you live."

The young princess, you may be sure, was not long in saying "Yes" to all this; and as they spoke a gay coach drove up, with eight beautiful horses, decked with plumes of feathers and a golden harness; and behind the coach rode the prince's servant, faithful Henrich, who had bewailed the misfortunes of his dear master during his enchantment so long and so bitterly, that his heart had well-nigh burst.

They then took leave of the king, and got into the coach with eight horses, and all set out, full of joy and merriment, for the prince's kingdom, which they reached safely; and there they lived happily a great many years.

Hush-a-Bye Baby

Hush-a-bye, baby,
On the tree top,
When the wind blows
the cradle will rock,
when the bough breaks
The cradle will fall:
Down will come cradle
And baby and all.

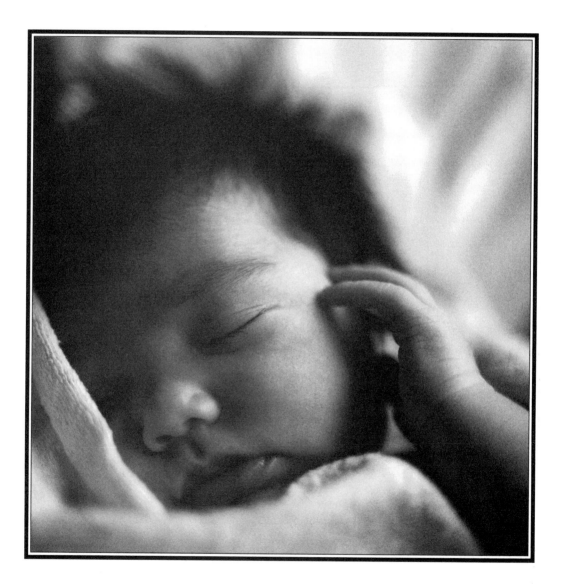

Sleep, sleep, beauty bright,
Dreaming in the joys of night;
Sleep, sleep; in thy sleep
Little sorrows sit and weep.

Sweet babe, in thy face
Soft desires I can trace,
Secret joys and secret smiles,
Little pretty infant wiles.

As thy softest limbs I feel
Smiles as of the morning steal
O'er thy cheek, and o'er thy breast
Where thy little heart doth rest.

O the cunning wiles that creep
In thy little heart asleep!
When thy little heart doth wake,
Then the dreadful night shall break.

—WILLIAM BLAKE

PART 3:

Recipes for Moms & Tots

RECIPE

Write down a recipe for a food you loved as a child that your mother or grandmother made for you. Pass it on to your children.

_____

_____

_____

_____

_____

_____

_____

_____

_____

_____

_____

_____

_____

_____

_____

Old Fashioned Chicken Noodle Soup

❖

1 whole chicken, washed and sectioned	2 teaspoons salt
3 quarts of cold water	$^1/_4$ teaspoon pepper
1 medium onion, chopped	1 bay leaf
4 celery stalks, chopped	$^1/_2$ teaspoon crushed thyme
1 cup of grated carrots	1 clove of garlic, crushed
3 chicken bouillon cubes	1 cup thin egg noodles, uncooked
2 tablespoons chopped parsley	

1. Combine chicken and water in large pot. Bring to boil and reduce heat. Skim any grease from surface.
2. Add onion, salt, thyme, bouillon cubes, garlic, bay leaf, and pepper.
3. Cover and let simmer for $1^1/_2$ hours.
4. Remove chicken from broth and let cool.
5. Remove skin and bone the chicken. Cut into small pieces and refrigerate.
6. Stir into broth the celery and carrots, and cook on medium heat for 20 minutes. Add in noodles for the last 10 minutes.
7. Add chicken and parsley.
8. Heat through and serve.

(Makes 8 to 10 servings)

Granny's Beef Vegetable Soup

❖

2 ¹/₂ pounds of beef, cubed	1 bay leaf
2 quarts of cold water	1 garlic clove, crushed
1 quart of V-8 juice	1 cup peeled and cubed potatoes
3 beef bouillon cubes	1 cup diced celery
1 ¹/₂ teaspoon salt	1 cup chopped onion
¹/₂ teaspoon crushed thyme or	1 cup diced carrots
¹/₄ teaspoon of marjoram	1 16-ounce can whole tomatoes,
2 whole allspice	undrained and cut
¹/₂ teaspoon pepper	1 ¹/₂ cups wide egg noodles

1. In large pot combine beef, water, and V-8 juice.
   Bring to boil and simmer 30 minutes.

2. Skim off any grease. Add bouillon, salt, thyme (or marjoram), pepper,
   allspice, bay leaf, and garlic. Cover and simmer for 2¹/₂ hours.

3. Remove meat and refrigerate. Add to broth all vegetables and simmer
   for 45 minutes. Add noodles the last 10 minutes. Add meat.
   Warm thoroughly and serve.

(Makes 8 to 10 servings)

Nanny O'Brien's Cream of Chicken Soup

1 whole chicken, washed and sectioned

3 quarts cold water

3 carrots sliced thin

4 stalks of celery sliced thin

2 medium onions, chopped

3 handfuls of long-grain, white rice

1 tablespoon salt

$^1/_8$ teaspoon pepper

1 tablespoon butter

1 tablespoon butter

1 12-ounce can of evaporated milk

4 tablespoons cornstarch mixed
   with cold water

1. Cover chicken with cold water and cook 1$^1/_2$ hours.
   (Bring to a boil and then simmer).
2. Remove chicken and cool. Remove skin, bone the chicken,
   cut into small pieces, and refrigerate.
3. To the broth add the carrots, celery, onions, chicken bouillon, salt and pepper.
4. Cook until the vegetables are tender (about 20 minutes on medium flame).
5. Add the rice and cook 10 additional minutes.
6. Mix cornstarch with cold water (just enough to make mixture smooth)
   and add to soup.
7. Bring to boil and boil for 1 minute.
8. Turn off flame, and add butter, evaporated milk, and chicken to the soup.
9. Heat until warm and serve.

(Makes 8 to 10 servings)

Mini Meatballs and Pinwheels

MEATBALLS

1 lb. ground beef	*1 teaspoon salt*
¹/₂ cup seasoned bread crumbs	*1 teaspoon pepper*
1 tablespoon chopped parsley	*1 egg*
¹/₃ cup water	*¹/₄ cup grated parmesan cheese*

1. Put met in bowl, set aside.
2. Beat egg with fork and add water, mix all seasonings
   with egg and add to ground beef.
3. Form mixture into small balls.
4. Place in sauce (see below) and cook for 1 hour on medium heat.
   (Can also fry meatballs until cooked through and place in sauce for ¹/₂ hour).

SAUCE

1 large can crushed tomatoes
(pureed in blender)
1 clove crushed garlic
1 medium onion, chopped
1 tablespoon parsley

1 tablespoon basil
1 teaspoon salt
1 teaspoon pepper
2 tablespoons olive oil

1. Sauté onion in olive oil until pearly.
2. Add garlic and cook until tender (do not brown).
3. Add tomatoes and all spices.
4. Cook over medium to medium low heat for 1 ½ hours.
5. Add meatballs to sauce (see above).
6. Cook pasta according to package directions.

(Makes 8 to 10 servings)

RECIPE

Stuffed Frankfurters

5 cups of cooked mashed potatoes

1/4 cup melted butter or margarine

2/3 cup onions, finely chopped

24 frankfurters

3 tablespoons prepared mustard

2 cups cheddar cheese, grated

6 slices of cooked bacon,
  crumbled (if desired)

1. Combine potatoes, butter, onions, and 1/2 of the cheddar cheese. Mix well.
2. Split frankfurters lengthwise without cutting all the way through.
3. Spread each frankfurter with mustard. Place in shallow pan.
4. Pile potato mixture in franks. Sprinkle with remaining cheese
   (and bacon if desired) and bake at 350°F for about 20 minutes.

(Makes 10 to 12 servings)

Easy Rice Pudding

❖

Use leftover rice or start	*1 large egg*
with 3/4 cup rice	*1/4 cup sugar*
1 1/2 cup water	*1 teaspoon vanilla*
1/2 teaspoon salt	*1/2 cup raisins*
milk	*cinnamon*

1. Combine rice, water, and salt in medium saucepan. Bring to a boil, cover tightly and reduce heat to low. Check after 10-15 minutes. Rice is done when all water is absorbed. Do not stir while cooking.

2. For pudding, cover rice with milk to about 1/4–1/2 over top of rice. Heat until milk is steaming.

3. In small bowl, beat egg with sugar. Slowly pour into rice and milk while stirring rapidly.

4. Continue cooking until mixture begins to thicken and is just about to boil.

5. Remove from heat. Stir in vanilla, raisins, and sprinkle with cinnamon

(Makes 6 to 8 servings)

Old Fashioned Animal Cookies

❖

1 cup shortening or butter (butter preferred)

2 ¼ cups granulated sugar

3 eggs

1 teaspoon baking soda dissolved in warm water

1 ½ teaspoons anise oil or vanilla

¼ teaspoon salt

3 cups sifted all-purpose flour

1. Combine butter and sugar. Add in eggs and beat until smooth.

2. Add baking soda, anise oil (or vanilla), and salt.

3. Slowly add flour, one cup at a time, and beat until smooth.

4. Chill dough in refrigerator overnight.

5. Roll out dough on floured board until very thin.

6. Cut out animal shapes with cookie cutters.

7. Place on greased cookie sheet and bake at 375°F until very light brown (5 minutes or so).

(Makes about 70 cookies)

Tasty Blueberry Squares

※

2 cups flour	$^2/_3$ cup milk
4 teaspoons baking powder	1 $^1/_2$ cups blueberries
$^1/_4$ teaspoon salt	$^1/_2$ cup sugar
5 tablespoons melted butter	$^1/_2$ teaspoon cinnamon

1. Mix flour, baking powder, and salt. Add butter, milk, and continue to mix.

2. Pour at once into greased pan. Press down until about $^2/_3$ inches thick.

3. Mix together remaining ingredients and spread on top.

4. Bake 12 minutes at 375°F.

5. Cut into squares and serve.

(Makes 36 squares)

Mom's Apple Pie

❧

PLAIN PASTRY

2 cups flour	*²/₃ cup shortening*
1 teaspoon salt	*5 to 6 tablespoons very cold water*

1. Mix flour and salt and sift together. Cut in shortening and add water while tossing until all dough is damp.
2. Separate in half and place in refrigerator at least 1 hour.
3. Roll out pastry thin on a lightly floured surface and place in 9-inch pie plate.
4. Roll out other half for top of pie. Set aside.

FILLING

7 cups of thinly sliced, peeled apples	*³/₄ teaspoon cinnamon*
³/₄ cups of sugar	*¹/₈ teaspoon nutmeg*
2 tablespoons flour	*1 tablespoon freshly squeezed lemon juice*
¹/₈ teaspoon salt	*2 teaspoons butter*

1. Preheat oven to 425°F.
2. In large bowl, combine apples and all ingredients except butter.
3. Place in pie crust and dot with butter. Moisten the edge of the crust with cold water.

4. Put top pastry over apples and fold top pastry under bottom pastry. Finish by pressing edges together with a fork dipped in flour.
5. To glaze top crust, brush with cream or slightly beaten egg white.
6. Make several small slits in top crust to let steam escape.
7. Bake for 40 to 45 minutes until apples are tender and crust is brown. (To test if done, insert knife into apples. Knife should pierce apples easily.)

(Makes 6 to 8 servings)

Yummy Popcorn Treats

❖

1 ¼ cups sugar   1 tablespoon butter

1 ¼ cups brown sugar   3 ½ quarts popped corn

½ cup light corn syrup   1 ¼ teaspoon salt

⅔ cup water

1. Combine sugar, brown sugar, syrup and water in a pot and place
   on medium flame.
2. Stir until all sugar is dissolved. Add butter and continue cooking, do not stir.
3. Cook until mixture forms a soft ball when tested in cold water
   (240°F on a candy thermometer).
4. Put popcorn in large bowl and sprinkle with salt.
5. Pour hot syrup mixture over popcorn and mix thoroughly.
6. Shape into small balls and wrap in waxed paper.

(Makes 15 3-inch balls)

RECIPE